Passive Income

How to Make Money Online by Blogging, Ecommerce, Dropshipping and Affiliate Marketing

(Wealth Using Real Estate And Online Business)

Stephen J Jackson

Published By **Bengion Cosalas**

Stephen J Jackson

All Rights Reserved

Passive Income: How to Make Money Online by Blogging, Ecommerce, Dropshipping and Affiliate Marketing (Wealth Using Real Estate And Online Business)

ISBN 978-1-77485-450-1

All rights reserved. No part of this guidebook shall be reproduced in any form without permission in writing from the publisher except in the case of brief quotations embodied in critical articles or reviews.

Legal & Disclaimer

The information contained in this ebook is not designed to replace or take the place of any form of medicine or professional medical advice. The information in this ebook has been provided for educational & entertainment purposes only.

The information contained in this book has been compiled from sources deemed reliable, and it is accurate to the best of the Author's knowledge; however, the Author cannot guarantee its accuracy and validity and cannot be held liable for any errors or omissions. Changes are periodically made to this book. You must consult your doctor or get professional medical advice before using any of the suggested remedies, techniques, or information in this book.

Upon using the information contained in this book, you agree to hold harmless the Author from and against any damages, costs, and expenses, including any legal fees potentially resulting from the application of any of the information provided by this guide. This disclaimer applies to any damages or injury caused by the use and application, whether directly or indirectly, of any advice or information presented, whether for breach of contract, tort, negligence, personal injury, criminal intent, or under any other cause of action.

You agree to accept all risks of using the information presented inside this book. You need to consult a professional medical practitioner in order to ensure you are both able and healthy enough to participate in this program.

TABLE OF CONTENTS

Chapter 1: What Really Is Passive Income? 1

Chapter 2: Reasons To Consider An Active Income Versus Passive Income 14

Chapter 3: The Things We Do To Love Each Other: How To Recognize Your Passion . 17

Chapter 4: Creating And Selling Apps 32

Chapter 5: Video Production 41

Chapter 6: Design And Set Up Blogs To Help People 49

Chapter 7: Reit (Trusts For Real Estate Investment) 51

Chapter 8: Passive Community Through Affiliate Marketing. 67

Chapter 9: The Stock Market 89

Chapter 10: Print-On-Demand 95

Chapter 11: Email Marketing 112

Chapter 12: Audio Books 118

Chapter 13: Defi (Decentralized Finance) 122

Chapter 14: Create Apps 150

Chapter 15: Passive Inside As Using "Time" 157

Chapter 16: Waiting For My Ship To Commence.. 167

Chapter 1: What Really Is Passive Income?

What does passive income mean and the way it is it earned? It is earning money without working to earn it, who wouldn't want it? Many dream of becoming wealthy quickly and attaining financial freedom. However, very few get it done. Anyone who believes they could make an enormous amount of money by making passive earnings in shortest time and with minimal effort is going to be disappointed. Because , with no effort there isn't any income to be earned. But, if you've got the patience and desire to become financially independent in the near future the passive income sources could be the perfect option for you. These will help you ensure your financial security in the near future. A passive income can be an excellent option for earning income specifically for self-employed and founders who are looking to earn an extra income in addition to their primary job. As long as you only work an hour or two each week, you could earn decent extra income as passive income. Passive income is typically described as money you earn when you're sleeping or taking a vacation, without needing to perform any. This isn't a complete nonsense also. However, it's often not mentioned the fact that you need to put in an enormous amount of time and effort before you can start. Then, you will get the chance to accumulate an income that is passive and reap the benefits of it. Contrary to the norm of a traditional occupation There isn't a clear connection between the time you work and earnings when you earn passive income. The major benefit is that you can earn more than the amount you earn without much effort. Even if you need to put in a lot of time and energy in the beginning, and likely only make a small profit from it however, the investment will be rewarded at a later time. It is possible to transfer money into your account, even in the event that you stop doing the work. The term"passive income" can be classified into two types which are: Portfolio income as well as external passive income. In the case of Portfolio income, specific quantity of funds are put into. A good example is to invest in stocks . But, that means you'll need some starting capital . The second option does not concentrate on the capital investment however, it is more about how much work needed to be completed. An e-book could be used as an illustration. We don't know when destiny will bring us to the future and whether or not we'll be able to complete the job we have been assigned until the time we become retired. Therefore, it is a wise objective to seek an income stream that is passive in the beginning. This way, everybody can ensure their financial security and earn an income that is passive. Financial independence is a goal which only a few individuals can attain. This is why we're introducing you to 25 methods in which you can earn passive income, as well as our top 10 strategies. However, we'd like to define what"passive income" actually means. Before we discuss the methods to earn passive income, we will define passive income and what it is that differentiates it from the work or active income. Then, we will discuss the 40 concepts that can be considered real passive earnings. Passive income is a recurring economic income that's not restricted by the individual's available time. In certain cases, it requires considerable effort or funds to establish the sources that produce it. Once they're established, they earn income without any intervention from their owners. Here is a link to the complete list of ways to earn income.

How does it work. We'll first take a examine the kind of income the majority of us earn : the active income . It doesn't matter if you're working for yourself or a self-employed business, you'll get paid to pay for the work that you've completed. In general, the following rule applies when you work: the more you exert yourself physically or mentally and physically, the more you'll earn. If passive income is the notion that it is created by itself, you do not have any or, at the very least, not to perform any work. There are a variety of ways to earn passive income. These include financial investments (in real estate, securities and so on.) or through sales of products (for for instance photo books or a book) or by renting your home. There is more information about the different possibilities of passive ownership later in the article. A lot of ideas involve any from the following.

Your concept is easily multiplied and sold as needed.

*The "operation" could be easily automated. This product, or product is not required to be maintained or / or upgraded, or even very

rarely.
* Your notion is timeless, or at the very least lasting.
* There is no competition. Can you earn passive income without the need for start-up capital?

The quick answer to the question whether you can earn passive income with no capital investment is yes, however. In the preceding paragraph, you must spend the time of your life or funds (usually both) in order to turn your idea into a genuine opportunity to earn income. If you plan to sell the product, it will need been planned, created and tested at least one time. A good example of possibly the "easiest to maintain" and the fastest way to make a product to earn an income that is passive is a picture which you can make available to download from websites to earn money. It doesn't require any money to do this, however you will need time. It is true that you may not make a fortune from it. Publishing and writing an ebook is significantly more expensive and time-consuming particularly at the beginning . If you are successful, you can expect to make a lot of cash. If you're short on time but plenty of startup capital it is possible to invest in securities (stocks bonds, stocks and bonds. as well as various types of investment funds) or real property. When you are investing in securities, there is virtually no time to invest other than maybe reading into the subject. This is why the financial investment is often regarded as the most pure type that passive earnings. This is because that the greater the initial investment capital is, the greater the potential passive income. However, based on the risks associated with investing, you may also lose lots of cash. Dos and don'ts of passive income Once you've discovered a good idea to earn passive income There are a few items you must consider. It is important to acquire the knowledge required by a professional. To manufacture an item, you require adequate abilities. If you don't have the skills then make it your own regardless of the some time. It is also possible to hire someone to handle the work on your behalf and charge you for the work. In addition, the expertise of a specialist isn't just useful when developing a new product idea as well as when it comes to investing in real estate or securities. It is important to know what you're investing you money for and understand how the market functions in the first place such as.

Only invest in what is essential. If you are currently in debt or other financial obligations make sure you take your time with them - even at least for the purpose of return before thinking about earning passive income source, such as through securities. There always is a chance of losing money through investments, and the funds should be for as long as it is possible to minimize the risk, never invest money that you will not require in your daily life. Be sure to tax the passive income. Like any other type of income, you are also required to pay taxes on your passive income. For example, rental income, on the profits from stocks or the sale of goods. Examine your ideas repeatedly. From the beginning, we emphasized that an idea for passive income should last as long as it is possible. However, very few people are so, make sure you make sure to check your plan frequently. This is the case for investing strategies within the market for capital as also to the relevance of the app you've developed.Don't take a break from your current job. It's not necessary, at least not immediately. If your dream of an income stream that is passive grows quickly, you must not rely solely upon an income that is active to earn money.

Instead, you should take a moment to think about whether you could reduce your work hours or if you are willing to start again with a new job or create your own company. Since the following is generally true an income that is passive will not make you rich or content. Do not fall for fraudsters who claim that you've got a secure passive income option by investing. When faced with attractive offers, make sure you think about the following question What if your friend has discovered a legitimate cash cow, why would they be willing to share this information with you? There are many other ways to make extra money. The opportunities we've given you for earning passive income share one feature in common: they require extensive preparation. They will most likely provide you with an extra income over the long run and you'll be a zealous advocate for it. Couldn't it be simpler? Are there any ideas you could use to make an immediate amount of money in order to increase your cash flow? The positive is that they are. But this isn't an issue of passive earnings, it's rather about earning based on the traditional exchange principle of performing for money. A whole industry has been developed under the name gig economy, which provides freelancers with temporary jobs. The term "gig" originates from the music industry and is used to describe short-term commitments for solo performances. This idea is applied to different industries businesses sign small, self-contained agreements with freelancers that do not result in an extended business relationship, or even an employee-related relationship. The arrangement usually occurs through one of the numerous Internet platforms which specialize in specific industries or services (e.g. for text messages, small IT jobs , or design projects). For design assignments, small IT jobs or text messages. UBER transportation service, as well as the diverse meals delivery options are part of this gig economy. If you're not able to fulfill any orders, or your business is dependent on fluctuating seasons, it might be beneficial to sign up using a platform that works for your needs. This way, you'll be able to earn money quickly and efficiently and also gain diverse experiences. But, the platforms will naturally want to make money, and that's why there are a limited number of opportunities to earn income. In the end your aim should always be to get orders from your customers on your own and to negotiate pricing and terms directly with your clients. However, there are many opportunities to generate income and also to add funds to your finances on short notice. Do you want to use your knowledge to offer tuition to students? The demand for tutoring is high, it isn't that expensive It's also satisfying to aid youngsters who have difficulties in school. If maths and German are not your forte You could also impart your knowledge of hobbies to other people: from spinning to DIY to cooking , the demand for courses that are appropriate is out there. Also, you can sell the products of your activities that you enjoy There's an audience for original gifts and handmade items. If you frequently travel on business, you might take passengers along on your journey. By doing this, you cut down on the cost of fuel and also meet a lot more people. There are websites to carpool, which act as mediators between demand and supply. This isn't a serious business idea, of course but sometimes every penny counts , and is beneficial for the environment as well. It's also the case with the second way in which you earn cash by doing second recycling of clothing as well as other preserved items. Clean up your mess and then dispose of the items you no longer require. Be it online or at the flea markets selling used items fills your pockets, relieves burden off your living space and also helps reduce the use of resources. It's clear that there are a lot more opportunities to earn extra money than you believe. Think creatively and consider ways to make use of the resources you have available to boost up your earnings in the near term. Consider all possible directions Do you have the ability to rent out rooms, machines, as well as other items? What are your strengths that others could profit from? Legal concerns Whether you have part-time work as tutor or invest in securities, or make money through online courses as a side hustle You must remember to report the earnings earned from these activities to your tax office. It is recommended to ask your tax office on how you must declare the additional income you earn and when it is necessary to tax it.

In certain situations it may also be beneficial to register your second venture as a separate company where you control your expenses and income in a separate manner. If you intend to earn income from your hobby selling your own products it is possible that you must adhere to the law, such as for food items or cosmetics. If you conduct commercial activities in the apartment you rent even if it's only for a weekend or if you lease the space for tourists to use, then you must get the permission of your landlord. It is also possible to sign up. Learn more about the rules in your area.

Passive income - conclusion tempting as earning money and not needing to do anything be, it's not so easy. Since, for most passive incomes, first you require the time or funds (or the two). Writing a book, or creating apps takes time and is rarely enough income that you are able to earn a living from home. Making investments in real estate or securities will require a sufficient amount of start-up capital, and there isn't a guarantee that you will earn a huge short-term gain afterward. Don't give yourself up with the aim of living on an income that is passive. Think of it as the chance to make some money to supplement your income and purchase additional time or a relaxing getaway or more flexibility when it comes to your daily decisions. this extra financial income.

Chapter 2: Reasons To Consider An Active Income Versus Passive Income

The benefits of considering the advantages of passive income over active income are just as numerous as the possibilities in Passive Income themselves. We are sure that the introduction may have caused you to think about the advantages of an approach to earning passively. But, in this section we'll shed deeper light on the top positive reasons to make money passively at any time.

Time: While passive income will require a significant time commitment to ensure it will produce its results. When you've created an efficient and long-term plan and the cash will begin rolling in quickly. This is similar to the wheel you spin initially, but after that it continues to spin independently. Thus, the investment of time can only be made once.

Money: Creating the foundation for a passive income stream requires for a minimum of even no investment. The resources you'll need to acquire to create and promote a product service that will generate a passive income are at your discretion typically. If it's not have a limit, it's available. You've got all

the resources it requires to create an income stream that is passive, in the event that you own any tangible asset that could or might not be directly beneficial to you, or any collection of knowledge, skills and talents or any other abstract resource that you could use to generate income. Thus, an investment in monetary terms could be insignificant when viewed in the larger perspective.
Convenience: As mentioned earlier posts, a good method of earning passively permits you to operate on your terms. It is possible that you will need to dedicate some time to establish your strategy after which, once it's running then you're able to relax and enjoy the flow of cash.
Alternative: This is a good reason to think about methods of earning passively. It is a fantastic alternative to live a financially sustainable life. While all of us have a way to earn an income regularly however, we may not be able to earn it for a long time even if wish to. The primary requirement for earning an active income is the ability to earn it consistently over both time and energy.
We'll get old in the future, and will have only a only a tiny amount of physical and mental capacity that we used to have. Our human

resources are limited and can limit our earnings. If you're over the age of 30, you'll fall frequently sick and, eventually, you're too weak to work a 9-5 shift or perform mental tasks for long periods of time. In the end, your boss dismisses you or advises you to quit your job. Sales drop when you're not able to stock the items in your store at the right time. What happens next? The money ceases to flow. What are you going to do to make an existence for yourself without your family? You struggle to meet your financial obligations to pay for groceries or utilities, and insurance and more.

What's the best way to proceed? You already know that. The next step is to choose another option that's nothing more than an income that is passive. The passive income, at this moment, won't be an extra wheel, but instead the steering wheel for your life. When you make the switch to a passive source of income, you'll be in a position to meet your needs and make handsome profits that will last for the duration the rest of your lives.

Chapter 3: The Things We Do To Love Each Other: How to Recognize Your Passion

One of the most effective types of passive income can be found from our passions. The reason why this is so vital is because passion is what propels you to move forward. Your passions will help you to work towards satisfaction. They'll help you carry on doing what you love, and while doing so, you will be able to enjoy your life.

As a young person What was it you always wanted to do? What was your favorite thing to do? Everyone has these in various types. Many people were interested in becoming musicians. Others wanted to be beauticians, artists, or even veterinarians. Many said they wanted to travel to the outer space, or discover dinosaurs, or construct objects for the purpose of earning making a living. There is no right answer to this question. Before we move on with our reading, take one second and consider what your younger version of yourself would like to accomplish. What did the younger version of you believe you would be doing when you were an adult? What did you tell yourself about throughout your life about what you could accomplish? There are many of us, so be truthful about it with yourself. There's a high chance that no matter what your answers is tied to your interests.

Your passions matter. They provide you with something that can be used to work from. They come up with something you can use as a basis to keep you engaged even when you'd rather be doing something different. Your passion is something that you have in the world that you consider sacrificing everything to pursue. A person who is passionate about art is not afraid to stay all late hours to work on their projects. A musician who is awed will commit endless hours in order to compose the perfect song, and then try to be a master of the art of. The writer who is passionate writes for hours in a trance state without realizing they've been writing for many hours.

It's not like working because we enjoy them in doing them. We are enthralled by the idea of creating those initiatives for our own enjoyment. We are always looking for the time and energy which we can devote to those things we love however, for the majority of us, we're told that our passions can't bring in wealth. The idea is that we could enjoy writing or painting or create anything else however, we are not going be able to pay for the expenses of doing it. Take a look at the comment and cliché about"the "starving artist." They dedicate their lives to their passions, but there's no money in it.

This isn't the situation. This is an assumption that people say. In reality that pursuing your passion is possible. You can earn money by following your passion. It is possible to let your passion assist you in creating the wealth you've always wanted in life. You could turn your passion into the career of your dreams. In no time you'll be seeing the wealth and benefits.

Finding your passion

Before you begin making money from your passion you must first identify what your passion is. Particularly if you've lived your entire life suppressing the things you enjoyed and then being warned that you will never achieve success, you may not believe it's an ideal idea to consider. Perhaps you've turned to avoid your interests believing that they're only for kids or for people who are scared of getting up. However, this is just society's attempt to make you to comply with its rules. Everyone has their own passions. Everyone has passions, even adults. However, they might have been suppressed. If you are able to identify something you love it is a good idea to take it to the next level. Once you've identified what you love and you are ready to pursue it to benefit yourself. This is why we're beginning by determining the things that you love to do. It could be whatever that you are interested in, and you shouldn't be embarrassed about what it is.

To discover your passion, you need to ask yourself a few questions. This kind of questioning introspectively will assist you as it allows you to discover areas of your personality which you might have hid through the course of your life. Start to ask yourself the questions and see what they lead you to. Keep in mind that even if you're unsure of which passions you're interested in then it's okay to have to try new things in order to discover the things you truly love. You may not have a clue at the moment, but you can discover it through trying different items. Let's start with the list of questions that you have to discover that spark that is within you:

* What do you enjoy doing?
* If you are free What are you researching?
* What causes you to lose the track of time so completely that you're totally in the moment? What's the thing that causes you to stop, look around and realise that it's been hours but you've never stopped to have a meal?
* What are you able to be talking about with others for hours on end without ever getting bored of it?
* If you were to remember three specific things following your death what would you

prefer for them?

* If you didn't have to work for a single day in your life, how would you do? What would you advise your self to be doing to make yourself content?

These questions aren't exact or precise however, they can help you think about what you need to do at every given point in the present. They will allow you to determine where you should be focusing. It could be that you realize that your passion lies in a place that you didn't think it could be. When you find it, you'll feel the joy that is derived from it. Once you've identified the passion is, then you can begin to concentrate on making money from it.

Monetizing Your Passion

Being able to make money out of your passion will depend on a number of important aspects which you must take care of. To begin, you must remember that in order to make your passion a profitable business you must be skilled. Skills are essential if you are hoping to implement a successful method of the process of monetization. If you're looking to make money from your passion, and you have the ability to do it then it's time to start.

If you've discovered your passion but don't have the skills it is essential to take the time to put it into practice. You must ensure that these skills are developed over time. If you're enthusiastic about writing, then practice! If you're awestruck by creating content, then you should do it! It is important to practice it to the point that it becomes automatic for you. If you continue to work as you progress you'll develop the skills you'll require. The abilities will be developed through repetition, and this repetition is essential in order to prepare you for creating the content.

Imagine you're obsessed with writing. Write every day, or at least often. You don't need to produce perfect content each day, however, if do not create content it's unlikely that you'll achieve much success. The masterpiece you've always wanted to create is waiting to be created however, you'll be unable to tell it's out there and you won't even know what the masterpiece is until it's actually made.

Once it's the right time after you've completed the training then you're ready to begin making money. It will depend on what you love to do. Are you passionate about the training of animals? You could offer your services to other people to earn money this way If you're happy in training others, you could begin recording and filming your method for this purpose which could ultimately become your own form of an income stream that is passive and relates to your love of animals as well.

Once you have identified the subject you are passionate about then you must decide what you're planning to produce to earn money. Are you creating books? Once you've honed your skills you can create books. You could also make instructional videos or vlogs on the subject. You could also start blogs. You can sell prints of your work , or even create music. There are a lot of options and once you begin selling something, you're able to make use of that item to earn the money you're seeking. If you are clear on what you want to make, you can begin thinking about your target audience. Who will you target? You will see people who clearly have specific targets. Certain people might target teens while others may be directed at adults. The book, for instance is mostly targeted towards women who are adults. I write for the things I've learned, since I'm writing for women, I write as if my readers are mature women that are probably working. That's after all, the audience! When making content, it is important to think about who your audience is and then ensure that you focus on that particular audience regularly.

When you've mastered the what and who, you can begin to address the method. Your content should be unique in some way or aspect which you can utilize. You shouldn't take someone else's concept and you have to create something that makes your content unique. It could be a motif within the material. Consider Vloggers. They generally include an intro and an outro to each video. These elements make it evident that it is a video produced by the individual. This allows your viewers to recognize your brand while making your work more consistent. This also allows you to move on to the next step: marketing.

Once you have a clear idea of what you're selling, you can begin marketing the product that you've wanted to put out in the marketplace. It is important for marketing be different for the person who is doing it. When you promote something, you'll be trying to make your product stand above what the competition offers. Also, you must make sure it's well-known, attractive, and can actually begin to draw in the customers you're hoping to reach.

Marketing is a subject which will likely evolve for you. It is essential to be flexible, especially when your business is growing ever more. Keep in mind that the goal is to build your brand's reach. It is important to ensure that your brand's image is growing bigger and more expansive so that you'll know that you have what you need. Consider ways you can grow. Consider ways you can improve the quality of content you decide to publish.

Always work to expand your business and get more people to know about your brand.

As you go about this, you'll need to ensure that you're making clear that you value your target audience. Of of course you will! Without your audience or customers there is nothing. This is something important to keep in mind if you are looking to earn money from your passion. Sure, a part of your goal is to make money however, remember that much more important than this, the goal is to spread your passion with others. Although money is nice and even important, is not the main thing. It is important to ensure that you are aware of that and make sure that you are able to cope with the reality. You must realize that you're doing this for a good motive. In the end, if all you were concerned about was cash, you'd likely continue working as a day-job! Most of the time, working in the daytime is easier than having to do the work to earn money from your passion.

The Reasons You Should monetize Your Passion

The best aspect of passions is that they allow

us to enjoy these passions. I love writing and am completely content to share my thoughts with you. Are there always butterflies and rainbows? Not at all. Editing? Not exactly fun. The pressure of writing? It can be difficult at times. But, talking about my thoughts and sharing my personal strategies to success to others is something I am passionate about. I am awed by the ability to share with others my experiences of the way I have gotten through life because I want to help other people to achieve success too! I look back at my current situation and consider, "Wow! I wish I had known someone who could have directed me to this area earlier!" It could have saved me so many hours. I would have jumped onto the wave of passive income faster if I had realized that I could live my life at home, without having the stress of my work. Naturally, I discovered the secret on my own and it's that feeling of longing for help from others that drives me to believe that I have a responsibility to be sharing my knowledge with others. Through sharing this information I'm helping others and possibly making a difference in someone else's life. The thought that I could potentially alter the lives of others through the words I compose is exactly what drives me.

The best part about passions is that you can make money from them in many different ways. This means that your interest according to what it is, most likely offers a variety of income you could earn. Although income shouldn't be the main reason for your passion however, if we're talking about how to make it monetizable you might want to maximize it in all methods that will help you succeed! Consider this: you can earn money by putting up videos and generating advertising income. There is also the possibility of sponsorships, based on what you are offering. It is also possible to begin to make money through your social media channels if you're big enough. You could write books about your content as well as offer tips to others wanting to start the same way as you do. You could begin streaming with a streaming service and earn money this is the best way. You can open an account on Patreon to collect donations. There are many ways to earn money.

The flexibility of this makes the pursuit of your passions a feasible option in terms of the monetization. If you are able to use these passions to earn income in a variety of ways, you are diversifying. Diversification is among the most essential aspects of income to keep in mind If you wish to make sure you're able to have this diversification is essential, you must find as many ways as you can earn cash. Making the income you want by doing something you love is among the most rewarding things you can do while paying your expenses. Once you've found identified a passion and you're ready to try to turn it into a profit in case you are skilled. Since it's something is something you cannot live without. Your passion is something you're motivated to do even when you're not paying for it, so why should you leave money lying around? If you're not making the most on the possibility that there is this money available and you're wasting the money. If you are planning to upload videos in the future then you must take the initiative to make money from the content. If you create books it is advisable to publish them. You never know, you could become the next famous person!

Chapter 4: CREATING and SELLING Apps

Mobile apps are those which can be downloaded and operated on smartphones. In 2017, over 400 million units were sold and the majority of them are used by Android. In 2015, app revenues were around 69 billion. This is projected to rise to 188 billion in 2020. If done correctly, can be an effective way to escape from the 9-5 wheel and bring closer to being financially secure. One of the major advantages of selling apps is that it is easily scalable. It is possible of reaching a huge population, and because people require great apps, just like any other good source of passive income and there is no requirement for maintenance once the majority of the work has been done. There are also obstacles to entry as creating an app is difficult work. This is why there are a lot bloggers since blogging is much easier than developing apps. This means less competition.

The easiest way is to turn your love for something into an app, no matter what it is. It doesn't matter if it's about cooking, dogs or computer games, or anything else it is possible for an app to be developed. It is possible to increase the amount of passion through the use of a suitable application. The apps can help to sort information more efficiently, while also collaborating with other individuals with similar interests, or even gamifying actions.

The idea of a project about your interest will give you a better chance because you will persist and persevere regardless of how difficult. In the event of a disaster you'll have some enjoyment. It is essential to be persistent because there are a lot of things to be learned before you can have your application gaining traction in any way.

In the beginning it is important to conduct your study and become aware of the other applications. The most effective apps have likely done something well. Do your research and discover the reasons for their popularity. You should think about ways you could incorporate some of their functions within your application without violating any kind of copyright. Look up applications that are relevant to your area and determine if a potential opportunity exists. Are there any gaps? Are your customers satisfied? Are there any areas you could improve on and make more the best value?

Start with a the basics. The more complex an application's design is the more challenging it can be to set up and even test. Your initial application should be simple, and is intended to be primarily an opportunity to learn.

The most basic applications are the ones that arrange details such as events, images, or illustrate how an activity can be done step-by-step.

The principal goal is to select an idea that is simple to develop into something that will generate an income that is passive for you. It is also important to design your application that doesn't require a great deal of maintenance. The best apps are those that require little more than minor periodic updates instead of one that requires many moving parts that work together. It is important to know how often updates must be made, the amount of testing is needed and how you'll be compensated, how feedback is received and communicated and in general how much involvement following the app's launch is needed.

The ability to make apps monetizable can be a means of earning money from the attention of others. Keep in mind that the single passive income stream isn't the only way to earn money. Multiple streams of passive income can be made from one app. You should develop your application with this in mind as re-designing it later could make it more likely to be prone to errors that could be costly. There are a variety of ways to implement the above ways of monetization. Some of them include in-app purchases as well as membership models, gift cards via platforms like Patreon or promoting your other products through the backend, or using the products of someone else , and thus being an affiliate marketing company.

Legal and regulatory guidelines such as trademark protection and GDPR are a crucial part of the process for creating an app. The investment in an expert in legal matters can save the company a lot of money and hassle later on It is essential to prepare for this as you, on your own, might appear as if legal professionals have a completely different language.

Your design and concept ideas should be first written on paper before taking any step. Begin brainstorming. The design may not be perfect the first time So be ready to try it again and over. It is important to include features and buttons that users will be able to see and interact with.

Applications must encourage interaction. The app should be designed to have a positive flow to earn passive income from it. Be aware of the ways that customers interact with your application and create it with the idea of passive income in the mind.

Before you begin developing, it's an excellent idea to create client stories. These are walks through of the user's actions within the app, and it is explained in detail how and why the app is utilized.

The product you offer should include the

reason the reasons why your application is selected. There are a variety of possibilities for USPs (Unique Selling Propositions) Some of them might be user-friendly that is bug-free, secure and battery efficiency.

You require a strategy to create an application that works. The plan must take tools and resources you'll require into consideration, the activities that must be completed and the people involved.

The ability to code is certainly beneficial as is having an idea for an application is a reason enough to learn how to code as it is a useful talent that can be beneficial in a myriad of ways. In any circumstance it is important to know the best way to become a programmer isn't a straightforward task however, if you believe that you're capable of doing it, then do it and study to become a programmer. Programming an app yourself provides users with a greater variety of choices and options which isn't always offered by an app creator software.

Instead of creating an application using code, you can use an app builder. It is easier because of the fact that it's less complex, and in general it is simpler and has less the potential for learning. You don't have to write only one line of code if choose to use an app builder this way. This is a feasible option for your initial design of your application.

The process of contracting a developer is expensive, and it's difficult to determine the exact cost because there will be changes made in the process and will affect the final price. It is still better off offering a fixed rate for this.

You must test your application for yourself. This is an essential part of the process because without sufficient testing, you cannot be sure that you are an advantage. You can test yourself however, you may also invite family and friends for a greater understanding. It is also possible to hire an expert to receive an objective evaluation. Testing can reveal potential bugs that could be present. When bugs are addressed the user experience of the app is able to be evaluated. Testers will surely give their opinions and can provide important information regarding the UX (User Experience). In the end, you need to determine ways to earn money from all this. Marketing is an essential part of. Without it, no one will ever hear about the app you have created. Advertising is basically about the education of your market what you can offer to their questions and concerns. There are several methods to promote an app. Create a simple way for your users to share your application with their colleagues. Make sure they have an incentive to act this. A great design that is simple to look at and a clear description of the app are the best ways to take. The reasons why an application is needed should be simple and appealing. General marketing strategies could include promotion of the app on websites such as journals online, Google, and social media. An income stream that is passive and steady can be earned from the sale of mobile apps. The combination of a high-quality design and a minimal maintenance is the important factor to create an income stream that will last for the long haul. It could take some experimentation and a few attempts to determine the most effective method, but you'll be richly rewarded in the event that you can persevere and be successful.

CHAPTER 5: Video Production

Do you enjoy making videos? Are you a video maker? Have you ever thought about how this passion could be turned into an income source?

The next chapter I'll discuss selling and marketing stock films, which are short videos that could be incorporated into commercials, TV programs or as components for other videos created by youTubers.

There is no special talent in art required, all you have to do is the ability to write the perfect content for this type of market.

The videos are licensed and sold under a license. for each one you can offer unlimited licenses for use, which means it's the kind of passive income that we are talking about in the book.

A professional camera is not needed

(although this will definitely improve how your video is produced) You can also create videos using a new smartphone (since they're equipped with high-quality 4K cameras). Selling stock footage does not require any special artistic abilities, but only a solid understanding of editing videos and managing light.

The movies you create can be uploaded to different platforms like Shutterstock as well as Adobe Stock where users purchase the right to use them for commercial purposes. This is known as "Royalty-free" When a buyer purchases a license use your film, but this film remains yours and is available to any person who buys the license.

In order to obtain an "royalty-free" license the video must not contain any elements that is protected by copyright. If there are any people in it, the publication of the film must be included with a statement of disclaimer about the use of the image for commercial use.

We have extensively analyzed the business model, therefore let's take a look at what steps are required to complete the business, which includes marketing strategies.

Phase 1 - Anaysis
We will employ a well-known analysis technique, which will analyze the search results made by people using websites for sales.

We can identify a subject or a video that is selling through the aesthetic manner used to create the various videos associated with specific subjects.
The topics that are always popular are the typical: technology, news videos, important life celebrations (weddings birthdays, celebrations, etc.) jobs, as well as videos about the people working, holidays and familymembers, etc.

It is possible that they all appear to be subjects that are very common however, adding your personal touches is crucial to add a distinct character to that topic.

PHASE 2 - Creazione contenuti e caricamento
Once you've decided on the topic of your video, you are able to begin to work on its creation.

Make short videos (5-30 minutes) If you have a long video you can cut it into smaller video clips and then upload each in a series. Although the video format is crucial, the formats most frequently requested formats are:

* 4K Video
* Time Lapse, or slow motion
* Shooting using drones
* 360-degree technology

After you have created the content after which you must upload them to various Stock Footage portals waiting to sell their licenses.

Your videos might not be approved,

particularly in the beginning of the business, but don't be discouraged, because you can use this opportunity to better analyze the videos. As time passes your critical abilities will develop and you'll better recognize a trend, and know how to make better videos. You should concentrate on the flaws in your competitors' videos in order to enhance your own.

PhASE 3 - Marketing

You could make stunning and flawless videos to the subject you've selected however if they're not displayed on the first page of results of your search, people are unlikely to view them. Furthermore, you cannot sell any rights to use.

The process is similar to those we'll look at in the following chapters in our book, therefore you'll need to improve the content you post to increase its SEO. If your videos are optimized for excellent SEO and are well-designed, your ad will appear prominently displayed on the first page of these searches.

More views you can get and the more you get, the better your chance of obtaining a license for use. When you buy more items, greater focus will be given towards the selling platform by placing your advertisement in results for that keyword. The chain reaction you trigger which will increase exponentially the number of sales you make from your videos.

PHASE 4 - Automate
The process of incorporating videos, titles and the description of it is an exciting step particularly when it is the very first time.

The creation of your first commercial is exciting. All publishing processes will personally be a part of the process for the first time and you'll be ecstatic to complete this. However, once your company begins to grow the processes will take away valuable time you'll require to study the market or create other videos.

Utilizing external services to complete these tasks is essential because they will save your time for instance, to speed up the loading process. It is possible to upload your video in their system and, with just one click they will then make sure that the video is distributed across all sales platforms. The loading process for your video at a low cost. You'll be able to see that the need increases as the quantity of videos that need to be uploaded rises.
They also provide additional services, such as editing video as well SEO optimization. Payment forms also include the formula for royalty share, by using this formula, you can will not pay a portion of future earnings in exchange for using these services. In this method you can lower the initial costs and the portals will earn a steady income for themselves. So when the video is successful it will earn you every one.

As you will see, this video is extremely funny It is a case of you taking a walk, you spot an interesting or specific event, and !... You film your video and then put it up in the marketplace, which means every opportunity that comes along is ready to be taken advantage of.

Chapter 6: DESIGN and set up BLOGS TO HELP PEOPLE

If you're skilled at creating or creating, you could create the look of a WordPress blog for other users and charge per hour for the services you provide.

It could cost you between $100 and more than $30,000 to construct an entirely functional WordPress website. And since you'd get the WordPress software free of charge A large portion of the amount you pay is your revenue.

The three main things you'll need pay for include your domain's name hosting as well as the WordPress theme. There are many other items that you'll need to run your blog, including extensions, plugins and banners that are designed are available for free, as there are more than 54,000 plugins that are available on WordPress.

The majority of the designers I have met were self-taught, and gained their education from tinkering around with WordPress open-source themes or watching paid and free videos that are available through YouTube, Udemy, or Coursera.

You can be a professional blog designer in only six months and begin earning money from this talent.

CHAPTER 7: REIT (TRUSTS FOR REAL ESTATE INVESTMENT)

Another way to invest on real estate to invest through REITs. They are essentially an array of real estate assets. Similar to how you'd have shares of the company's stock, you'll have shares of commercial properties like flats, office buildings, or malls.

REITs (real estate investment trusts) are an essential part of any equity or fixed-income investment portfolio. They provide more variety as well as higher total returns and/or lower risk overall. In short, their ability to earn dividends while also increasing their value makes them a great supplement to bonds, stocks as well as cash.

The properties or mortgages that are secured on these properties Real estate investment trusts manage and/or hold commercial real estate that generates income. If you are an individual, via an exchange-traded funds or an investment fund that is mutual, you are able to put money into the companies. REITs are available in a range of sizes and shapes.

Reit Historical Returns

Investment trusts in real estate have been historically one of the most lucrative types of assets. Investors typically use this FTSE NAREIT Equity REIT Index to gauge its performance in the US real property market. The index posted an average annual performance of 9.5 percent from 2010 to 2020.

In the last few months, from November 2017 until November of 2020, the three-year mean of REITs was 11.25 percent, significantly more than that of the S& P 500 and Russell 2000, which were 9.07 percent and 6.45 percent respectively. Investors who seek yield have traditionally performed better as opposed to fixed income, the standard asset class, and for this reason. Both are worthy of consideration in an investment portfolio that is well-planned.

1. Retail REITs

Shopping malls and retail stores make up about 24percent of REIT investment. 3 . This represents the largest investment made in America by type. Every mall you visit is likely to be operated by an REIT. If one is considering a real estate investment, one must first look at the retail sector. Are they financially stable and what is the outlook of the coming years?

It's important to remember that retail REITs earn revenue through the cost of renting tenants. If a business is experiencing difficulties with cash flow because of lower sales, they could be forced into bankruptcy if they don't pay rent in time or on time. Renters for a new tenant must be found in that moment which is not easy. Therefore, it's crucial to invest in REITs with the most reliable anchor tenants. Businesses in home and kitchen improvement as well as grocery are just two examples.

After you've analyzed the market then you need to focus on the REITs in themselves. It is crucial, as with any investment, to ensure they're profitable, have solid balance accounts, and as much as possible in debt, especially short-term debt. Retail REITs with substantial capital reserves will be provided with opportunities to buy appealing real estate at bargain prices during a downturn. This can be a profit for the most well-run companies.

However, there are more long-term issues facing the retail REIT industry as shopping is shifting on the internet instead of through malls. Space owners continue to develop new ways to fill their premises with offices and other tenants that are not retail However, the industry is in trouble.

2. Residential REITs

They can be described as REITs (REITs) which own and manage multi-family rental complexes as well as prefabricated houses. Before investing in this type of REIT there are a few points to be considered. The most desirable apartment markets, as an example ones where home prices are affordable compared to the rest of the nation. The cost of single homes in cities such as New York and Los Angeles encourages more renters to live in the area and increase the rent that landlords might need to charge. This is why the biggest REITs that deal in residential properties tend to concentrate on the major metropolitan areas.

Investors must look for the employment and population growth in every market. If there is a net flow of people into the city, it's typically because jobs are plentiful as well as the economic sector is growing. The combination of a decreasing rental rate and an increasing vacancy rate indicate that demand is increasing. Residential REITs will be successful in the long run, as long as the unit supply in the area is restricted and demand continues to grow. They have the best balance sheets as well as the most available funds, similar to other companies, typically do the best.

3. Healthcare REITs

As people age and healthcare costs increase the healthcare REITs will become an important subsector to watch. Hospitals, medical centers nursing homes, as well as retirement homes are among the assets which healthcare REITs invest in. The growth of real estate is tightly dependent on health care systems. Fees for occupancy, Medicare and Medicaid payments along with private money are the main sources of funding for the majority of these institutions the owners. Healthcare REITs are likely to remain a mystery in the event that healthcare funding is not certain.

A diverse set of customers, along with investments in various properties, are some of the factors to consider in the healthcare REIT. To a certain extent the focus can be beneficial however, so is spreading the risk. A increase in the demand for healthcare services (which is expected to be expected as the population gets older) can be beneficial to health real estate. In addition to property and customer kind of properties, search for companies with extensive healthcare experience and strong balance sheets and access to affordable financing.

4. Office REITs
Office REITs are businesses which make investments in offices. Tenants who have signed long-term leases pay them rent revenue. If you are thinking of investing in a REIT for offices There are four issues that come to mind.
What is the current state of the economy? And what is the unemployment rate?
* What is the current rate of vacancies?
How is the current state of economic activity in the areas in which it invests? REIT invests?
* How much has it set aside to purchase items?

Find REITs that invest in hot economic areas. A collection of subpar structures located in Washington, D.C. is better than owning a top office properties in Detroit such as.

5. Mortgage REITs
Mortgages comprise about 10% of the assets of REITs and are a far cry from actual real property. 3. Fannie Mae and Freddie Mac companies that are government-sponsored and acquire mortgages through an auction market are among the most popular, but they are not always the most profitable investment.
But just because an REIT has a stake in mortgages more than equity doesn't mean it's safe. A rise in interest rates will lower the value of the books of mortgage REITs and cause their the prices of their stock to drop. Mortgage REITs also have to raise an important portion of their capital via secure and non-secured debt. The future borrowing is more costly because interest rates are rising and reduce the value of a portfolio of loans. Mortgage REITs typically are traded at a discount to the net asset value of each share, in a low interest rate situation, but with the potential for rising rates. Finding the right one is the most difficult thing.

The Essentials for Assessing Any REIT
When looking at any REIT there are several

aspects to keep in mind. These are just a few of them:

The real estate trusts (REITs) are true investment options that provide total returns. They can provide significant dividend yields, as well as small, long-term capital gains. 4 Search for firms that have a track record of providing both.

A lot of REITs, in contrast to conventional real estate, trade through stock exchanges. The benefits are diversification in real estate without being tied in for the duration of time. Liquidity is essential.

Depreciation can increase the value of a property. Instead of focusing on the payout ratio of a REIT (which is what dividend investors use) examine the fund from operations (FFO). It means net income less depreciation, and any property sales during the year in question. Dividing the dividend by FFO in order to determine what is the FFO/share. It is better to earn a higher rate.

It is important that you have a good management. You should look for companies which have been in operation for some time or, at the very minimum, have a seasoned management team.

It's all about the high-quality. Make sure to

invest only in REITs (REITs) that have excellent rental and assets.
Think about investing in REIT-focused mutual funds, or exchange-traded funds (ETF) instead of leaving buying and research to experts.

Advantages and disadvantages of REITs
Like other assets offer advantages and disadvantages. High yield dividends are among the most appealing aspects of REITs. REIT dividends tend to be much higher than the average company in the S&P 500.5 because REITs are required to pay 90% of the tax-deductible earnings to shareholders. Diversification of portfolios is another benefit. Many people do not have the money to purchase commercial real estate generate passive earnings, However, REITs allow people with the possibility of doing that. Additionally, while buying or selling property may take a lot of time which can result in cash flow being slowed REITs are highly liquid and a majority of them available to purchase and sold at one click button.
There are a few disadvantages of REITs that investors must be conscious of, the most important of them being the tax burden REITs

could trigger. Since the majority of REIT dividends don't meet what the tax authorities consider to be "qualified dividends" REIT dividends can be taxed an increased rate than other dividends. While REITs are eligible for the pass-through deduction, the majority of investors are required to pay significant taxes on REIT earnings when they hold them in the traditional brokerage account.

The potential vulnerability that REITs with regard to rates of interest is another risk. REIT prices tend to decline in the event that they are impacted by the Federal Reserve raises interest rates in an attempt to control on spending. Additionally, various forms of REITs have specific risks to properties. For instance, hotel REITs typically perform poorly in economic downturns.

Pros
* Dividends that have high yields
• Diversification in your portfolio
* Extremely liquid

Cons
 Dividends are taxed at same rate as income that is ordinary.
* Sensitivity to interest rates

* Certain traits have risk associated to them.

Risks associated with Real Estate Investment Trusts
REITs typically offer a higher yield than the market because they pay at minimum 90 percent of their tax-deductible earnings to shareholders. Dividends, or cash dividends paid by businesses to their shareholders and are the method REITs use to give their investors. While many companies offer dividends to shareholders, REITs offer greater dividend returns than other dividend-paying businesses.
REITs are required to pay dividends to shareholders for 90% of the tax-deductible income. Therefore, they typically pay more than other dividend-paying corporations. Certain REITs are specialized in a particular real estate market, while others offer a wider portfolio.

A variety of different kinds of properties are held by REITs. These include:
* Apartment building
* Healthcare establishments
* Hotels
* Offices are housed in buildings

* Self-storage facilities
Malls are an example of shopping centers.

REITs appeal for investors as they offer an opportunity to earn dividends from these investments having no ownership of any. That is to say, investors don't have to put in the money and effort required to buy an investment property that could lead to unexpected expenses and difficulties.
It's easy for investors to believe that If the REIT has a strong management team, a proven track of performance and exposure to desirable assets, investors can just sit and watch their profits increase. However, they have a number of weaknesses and risks that investors must be aware of prior to making any investment decision.

Risks of REITs that are not traded
Non-traded REITs, often referred to as non-exchange traded REITs are at risk because they do not have a listing on a stock exchange.

Share Value
Since non-traded REITs cannot be publically

traded as such, investors are unable conduct research about them. This means that finding out the value of the REIT's assets is a challenge. While some REITs that are not traded are required to disclose all their assets and values within 18 months it isn't always the case.

Lack of liquidity
Non-traded REITs also aren't liquid and, therefore, when investors want to sell, it might there be no buyers or sellers on the market. REITs that are not traded, in certain circumstances, are not sold for at minimum seven years. Certain REITs, however, allow investors to take a percentage or all of the investment within a year, for a fee.

Distribution
Non-traded REITs need to pool funds to buy and manage properties, thus securing the funds of investors. The pooled funds, however can have a dark aspect. The darker side happens the case when a property pays dividends from investors' money instead of profit that the property earns. This can reduce the cash flow of the REIT and reduces the value of its stock.

Fees

Fees for upfront are another drawback of REITs that are not traded. Most require an advance charge of between 9 and 10 percent and some charge up to 15 percent. One can find instances where non-traded REITs are able to manage their assets and properties that result in huge profits, however this is also the case for REITs listed on the public market. Fees for external managers are feasible in REITs that are not traded. External management is paid for by an REIT that is not traded and can reduce investor returns. If you choose to invest in a non-traded REIT be sure to inquire about all pertinent concerns regarding the risks discussed above. The more transparency the greater.

Risks of REITs that are publicly traded

REITs that are traded publicly give investors the chance to add real estate into their portfolios, while earning healthy profits. While REITs that are listed publicly are more secure than non-exchange REITs however, there are risks.

Risk of Interest Rates

The most significant risk to REITs is an rising interest rate which reduces demand for REITs. Investors typically prefer safe yield bets, such as U.S. Treasury bonds, in a rate-soaring environment. Treasuries. Treasury bonds are guaranteed by the government and pay a predetermined percentage of the interest. This means that as interest rates rise REITs fall and the market for bonds rises because money flows into bonds.
However, higher rates of interest could be taken as an indication of a strong economy, resulting in higher rental and occupancy rates. But, REITs have generally been underperforming when interest rates rise.

The wrong REIT to choose
Another risk is choosing the wrong REIT. This may seem easy, but it's all about logic. Malls in the suburbs, for instance have seen a decreasing side. Therefore, investors might be wary to invest in REITs with exposure to suburban malls. Urban retail centers could be the best investment option for those who are millennials and prefer city life for its ease of living and savings on costs.
As trends shift It's crucial to review the REIT's assets and properties to make sure they're

relevant and capable of producing rental income.

Tax Treatment

Although it is not an inherent risk in its own, the fact dividends from REITs will be taxed like regular income could be an important factor for certain investors. To explain it in another way. the regular tax rate is identical to the rate of tax on income for investors that is probably higher than the dividend tax rate or capital gains tax rates for stocks.

The investment in REITs (REITs) could be an investment with low risk and high return to buying the property directly. The large dividends that REITs pay out should not convince investors as REITs could be underperforming markets in rising interest rate environment.

CHAPTER 8: PASSIVE COMMUNITY through affiliate marketing.

Consider gaining more financial freedom to travel or enjoy an easier life at home for a while. If this seems like a dream It doesn't have to be. You can land yourself in a position similar to this by earning affiliate revenue even if you're not making progress.
What does Affiliate Income mean?
What do you mean by affiliate earnings? It's the cash you earn through affiliate marketing. Through an affiliate marketing program you earn money through marketing other people's products or services.
Common methods to advertise affiliate income programs are to use advertisements that display (such in banners) as well as links and subjects.
Affiliate Marketing Average Earnings
Want to know what an average total affiliate marketing salary? The statistics vary, affiliate marketers can earn hundreds of dollars. The most successful earns six figures from affiliate programs that generate passive income.
Here are some statistics on the average income of marketers who are affiliates. According to PayScale, the median annual

passive income earned by affiliate marketers is $51,217. The lowest 10% from affiliate marketing earns $37,000 and the top 10 % make $71,000.

The statistics on affiliate marketing's income from Glassdoor reveal that the potential earnings can be even greater. Affiliate marketers make an average of $65,800 annually and salaries range from $42,000 at the lower end, to $83,000 at the top end. With a total annual income of $154,700, ZipRecruiter has the highest estimate for passive affiliate marketing income. According to ZipRecruiter's estimates, the average monthly earnings from affiliate marketing is $12,892, while the average weekly income is $2,975.

No matter what predictions you trust regardless of which forecast you believe, there's no doubt that certain Affiliate marketers have been doing extremely well.

Blog Revenue comes from Affiliate Marketing

A blog that earns affiliate income is a vital instrument for any potential affiliate marketer. Blogs are efficient in the generation of affiliate revenue for the exact reasons that they work in business:

* You are regularly updating material that you

can use to expand your reach.
You can do this via natural traffic or email marketing or paid-for promotions, you are able to reach an extensive public.
It's easy to include affiliate-related content, regardless of whether it's content or links to promote.
* In the process of creating relevant content over time, you will establish your authority. Many affiliate marketers make thousands of dollars each month via their blog. In just one month, for instance:
* Helen was paid more than $3,600.
* Ryan Robinson made over $44,000.
The sum of more than $80,000 was the prize won from Adam Energy.
* Other bloggers earn more by creating an affiliate-based blog can pay off for them.

Passive income from Affiliate Marketing

A lot of people are not sure of how to handle the "passive" element of affiliate marketing in order to earn money online. However, it's not as easy as "post an advertisement and connect with people." Making money takes constant effort.
In truth it's going to take into setting up your blog, select the right partner income service and create material to promote these

services. If you've have it set up properly it shouldn't be necessary to do anything further especially if you already have any content that has been optimized for evergreen. Selecting the best affiliate program is another aspect that can assist you in earning passive affiliate earnings.

Affiliate Programs that Offer the highest residual income

If visitors to your website make a purchase the product, many affiliate income program offer a one-time payment. If, however, you really would like to earn passive income, search for affiliate programs that are high-end. They allow you to earn regular affiliate commissions in a streamlined method. Following a sale, you can receive commissions for an agreed-upon time period like one year. However some plans allow you to earn monthly payments for the remainder the duration of your existence.

Affiliate Programs that Pay the Most Recurring Commissions

Here are a few of the top affiliate programs that generate an income stream that the top affiliates suggest.

1. Social Pilot is a social media management platform.

Social Pilot, a social media automation tool, provides an affiliate income program that is free. Every new referral earns an additional 30% of the commission which will be doubled with every renewal.

2. Lead Pages is a website that lets you create landing pages.

Lead pages has a generous affiliate income program to its software for lead generation. Affiliates receive 50% monthly payments throughout the life of they refer clients they refer to them with Lead Pages.

3. Weebly is a site which lets you build your own

Weebly, along with the majority of income plans for partners, charge a monthly fee of 30% for the purchase of tools to build websites.

4. Weber provides an email marketing service.

Weber Advocates are part of Weber's partnership network, which offers email marketing. If your customers are your referrals they can join for no cost and earn an annual 30% commission.

5. Convert Kit is a conversion tool that runs on the web. tool.

Anyone who is knowledgeable about the

importance of email marketing should make use from Convert Kit's affiliate revenue program. Join for free and receive an annual 30% payment for in the event that your customers you refer stay in Convert Kit.

5 Tips to Increase Your Affiliate Revenue

Are you looking to become an effective affiliate marketing success? Here are our top ideas for earning a monthly passive income.

1. Choose the Right Product

Do not give in to the desire to become an affiliate for all things. Instead, focus on promoting products you are familiar with and enjoy and also those which are relevant to the people you want to reach. If you can make your offerings are the more likely people who come to your website will click through those links, which will generate an income stream for you.

2. Provide relevant information

The traditional sales pitch isn't as effective. People want reliable information that allows them to better understand the products and services they use and make their own choices. The most effective affiliates publish product reviews guidelines, comparisons, and guides that aid their readers and establish confidence.

3. Optimize Your Content

After you've composed your content Make sure that it's optimised to make it easy for people to locate it on search engines. The number of searches for product reviews continues to grow. In the event that your affiliate advertising appears on the results page this makes it more likely that you'll get an income.

4. Make use of video for promotion

Buyers on the internet are seeking reliable information. In fact, 55% of customers make use of video when shopping in stores. Video footage of the user how to use the product or reviewing it will can be a great way to get the word out. You might consider the use of video as part of your affiliate marketing methods for promotion.

5. Try to Boost Conversions

The process of attracting visitors towards your affiliate revenue website is not the only hurdle to overcome. The next challenge is to get users to click. One method to increase your chances is to play around using your headlines as well as calls to actions. One way to accomplish this is to use Taboola's Title Analyzer , which can determine the likelihood of CTR that your headline will generate.

You can also check out trends for videos and images to determine what will attract your viewers the most. For instance, if you're marketing technology across the United States, images without people have a 26 percent better CTR than images with people.

4.1: Affiliate Marketing Promotion Techniques

While affiliate marketing may aid in increasing sales and interaction but it's not enough to simply unleash advertisements and expect the best.

The organic presence on websites like Facebook and Instagram is declining for a variety of publishers and labels. This means that earning profits from affiliate marketing isn't quite as straightforward as creating content of high quality and then selling it on the spot. In order to draw traffic to your advertising and affiliate marketers you'll need to have the right methods of outreach and content.

We've created an inventory of the best 9 affiliate marketing marketing strategies and strategies to help you boost the amount of affiliate marketing income you earn:

*PPC (Pay Per Click)
* Blogs on social media and SEO
* Coupons for How To Videos

* Reviews for webinars on email marketing

How will Affiliate Marketing be Promised?
Make use of these affiliate marketing promotion methods to boost the number of people who are exposed to the advertisements of affiliates.

PPC Pay-per-click (PPC) advertising involves placing ads in web pages or in search results for clicks. The advertiser paysfor the clicks, and the site hosting or publisher earns a profit each time a customer clicks the PPC advertisement.

E.g. for instance, for instance, a Google lookup of "fall boots" will return results that are organic followed by results that are supported - or PPC ads.

Taboola is also a great tool to use for PPC promotionssince it lets marketers target users through premium publisher platforms with recommended content and videos that result in sales.

Utilization of Social Media

Advertisers will be able to reach millions of users worldwide through social media websites which are eager to know more about their favourite brands and products. Based on the Global Web Index, almost 50% of adult Internet users conduct product testing through social media platforms. Affiliate marketers must share their content, create an following and be involved in the latest discussions on social media platforms such as Facebook, Instagram, and Twitter. Customers can buy items directly from their channels due to the social ads features, which means they don't need to leave their mobiles to purchase.

SEO or Search Engine Optimization (SEO)
SEO or Search Engine Optimization (SEO) helps make websites more accessible to people who use their services. Your chances of appearing in search results -- as well as attracting users looking for what you've got to say by utilizing a variety of familiar keywords that can be searched in your content, images, tags and metadata.

Organic search traffic rose by 53% across all sectors in 2019, as per BrightEdge research. This was faster than other platforms, such as social networks.

Blogging
Blogging is among the most effective methods to help companies promote themselves through affiliate marketing. The blog you start will aid in building credibility within your field and establish yourself as the go-to source for

important information, and increase an audience that comes back to read more. Take, for example, affiliate marketer GoPro. Their website, The Inside Line, their site is a look into the most current news and "what's happening within the world of GoPro."

Educational Videos

Internet consumers are inundated with social and online content as well as live streams, which are driving up the amount of online video watched. According to Zenith the average person spends on average 84 minutes every day on the internet watching videos, and that number is expected to increase to 100 minutes in 2021. Between 2013 and 2018, online video streaming was up by 32 percent in average.

Affiliate marketers can use online video to market new products, host Q&A sessions or reach out to specific markets, and even give live demonstrations, providing immersive and visually captivating possibilities for prospective customers.

Gear Patrol, for example makes use of the YouTube channel to look in the companies it recommends as well as reviews by associate brand partners.

Coupons

Everyone appreciates a good bargain. In actuality that 97 percent of shoppers look for bargains, and 92 % are still searching to find the lowest price.

Offer exclusive discounts and offers specific to their interests in order to convince potential clients to join their ranks or to thank customers who have been with them for their loyalty. RetailMeNot, Offers.com, Honey as well as Tec Bargains are some of the most well-known discount sites for affiliate marketers.

Email marketing

More than 3.9 billion email subscribers worldwide and the number is predicted to increase to 4.3 billion in 2023. A majority of B2B marketers believe that email newsletters as the most effective lead-generating tool. It's unsurprising. Advertisers and brands will be sending personalized content directly to users' inboxes by email, which is an opt-in option.

Mail marketing can be used to exchange personal offers, promote popular blog posts, or direct users to the product's website. Bombast is an online retailer, does a fantastic job at this through the delivery of regular newsletters that are tailored to the audience's desires.

Webinars are another option.

Webinars, which include in-person sessions and seminars, aid advertisers in engaging with their clients personally and provide a greater insight into their services. They're still in a position to encourage participants to sign up for email notifications at the time of registration and to keep in contact with them after the event has concluded.

As per Go to Webinar, email is the main driver behind more than 57 percent of webinar registrations as well as 67 percent of webinar registrations, providing an opportunity to make contact with consumers.

Evaluations

A business -- and even an affiliate marketing strategy can be built or destroyed by customer feedback. Think about this: over 91 % of customers are able to read online feedback and 84 percent consider them more than personal guidance.

It is crucial for marketers who are affiliates to keep an eye on the performance of their Google as well as Yelp review pages, listening to the feedback of customers and making discounts for leaving reviews. Marketers can also work with associate publishers who write product reviews and offer personalized links for users to click and purchase.

4.2 The Top Dating Affiliate Programs

Everyone is looking for love online, and it is among the most sought-after ways. With over 1500 dating apps and forums that are eager to connect users online, dating on the internet is an attractive field for partners marketing specialists.

Since dating services are able to offer high rate of conversion and are also free that affiliate marketers can earn an enormous amount of money from advertising these products. This article will focus on the top-paying affiliate dating sites and the most efficient campaign methods to implement.

Affiliate Programs to help with Dating

• Affiliate Program with Cougar Life for Dating
"Affiliate Program" for Match Dating
"Cupid Media's Affiliate Programme for Online Dating
* eHarmony Dating Affiliate Program is an affiliate program that lets you get paid by referring others to

Partner Program with Silver Singles Dating Affiliate

The affiliate programs with the highest payouts are listed above then the lower earning affiliate programs. The amount you can earn and the specific benefits every program has are the two primary aspects to take into consideration when selecting the most appropriate products to market.

The program's activity

You'll be able access to many different advertising creatives to use for show banners as well as social and search PPC promotion, as well as much more after you've been approved. You'll save lots of dollars since a monthly subscription cost is way too expensive.

The Registration Procedure

Complete a short questionnaire on the website of the company for questions regarding routes and duration of traffic.

Highlights from Using the Software

Cougar Life has a mobile-friendly application as well as high commissions. Support is available around all hours of the day.

Commission rate of 80 percent

The typical fee (per purchase) will be $32 for a month of subscription.

Incomplete EPC (earnings per 100 clicks).
Cookie life span: 30 days
The program's activity
The match is the world's most well-known dating site, with 30 million monthly visits. The three-month minimum membership agreement gives out a large amount of commissions. If you're a top member and you're a top partner, you'll be able to get special coupon codes that will can help you get more leads. In addition, you could earn 25 percent more.
The Registration Procedure
Commission Junction or Rakuten Advertising are two ways to join an affiliate program.

Highlights from the program's use
Match is staffed by a dedicated team of outreach willing to assist you. Match also gives additional prizes contingent on the results.
A commission of 75%
In a three-month subscription for a 3-month subscription, the average commission (for the sale) will be $42.
$18/3 month EPC (earnings per click)
Cookie life span: 120 minutes
The Activity of the Program

Cupid Media welcomes everyone to join its network of partners and provides posters and text connections to affiliates for make use of for their marketing. It hosts 35 specially designed dating sites that are used by millions of people.

The Registration Procedure

Register on the company's website an agent will get in touch with your within the next 48 hours. Accepted

Highlights of the use of the program

If someone signs to sign up for a free account you earn commissions and the customer service is helpful.

Commission rate of 75 per cent

For a one-month subscription, the typical fee (for sales) will be $19.50.

The unknown EPC (earnings per 100 clicks).

Cookie life span: 30 days

Harmon is an electronic music company. music.

The Activity of the Program

Because eHarmony is most trusted dating site It's easy to get people to join. You'll be able to access frequently up-to-date promotional materials as well as exclusive offers until you've been accepted. Affiliates are considered to be long-term associates of the company and are ready to support you in your achievement.

The Registration Procedure

Commission Junction is where you can sign up for the service.

Highlights of the program's use

It's simple to promote, gives affiliates with exclusive deals and offers a variety of top-performing creatives.

The commission rate is 20%..

For a subscription of 3 months for a 3-month subscription, the median commission (per sold) will be $34.

$82/3 month EPC (earnings per click)

45-day cookie length

Silver Singles is a dating site for those who are single and over

The Activity of the Program

Silver Singles is different from other options in that it is paid per lead. It is a benefit that you receive a regular payment regardless of the length of time the client is enrolled. The website caters to professionals who are over 50. So this program is a great choice for the audience you want to reach.

The Registration Procedure

To join, visit CJ Affiliates.

Silver Singles offers a pay-per-lead cost and offers members highly-converting campaigns to advertise.

$7 commission fee

For each sign-up that is completed for sign-up, the commission average (per purchase) of $7.

45 EPC (earnings per 1,000 clicks)

Cookie life span: 30 days

Why should you participate to participate in Affiliate Programs for Dating?

The most profitable areas to earn cash is dating online. The desire for love is a fundamental human desire, making it an evergreen industry. People who are looking for a partner are looking for the most recent dating websites, dating advice and discussion starter lists available on the internet. I'm sure you've got the concept. You'll have the best chance of success if you supply the necessary items.

Affiliate Programmes For Dating: How to Advertise They

Once you've determined which dating service to market, you'll need to create and implement an effective marketing plan. In order to ensure that you're able to keep clients, you should consider converting them using the combination of tried and true methods of digital marketing.

Marketing Content

You'll need a blog when you're an affiliate marketer in order to host everything you have to offer including images, posts podcasts, images, and the list goes on. Top 10 lists as well as how-to content are examples of top-performing content, however the topics you select should be representative of the interest of the readers. Be sure that the material can be searched and also monitor headlines to determine which are most popular with readers.

User Experiences

The stories of happy customers inspire us and 92 percent of customers read reviews before making purchases. By incorporating testimonials into blog posts or landing pages you'll allow them to perform the heavy lifting for you.

It is the Internet and Social Media

Dating is a social event as well as 83.36 percent of online users utilize Facebook and Twitter, sharing content of these websites can help you reach an extensive crowd. People who are younger in their dating choices

TikTok and Instagram and older users prefer Facebook. It's also important to look past the big users and look into sites like Quora as well as Reddit. The right photos are essential to get an individual's attention and attracting attention, so be patient.

Create campaigns

Paid-for campaigns are a great option to attract highly targeted quality, highly targeted visitors to your site. By combining techniques for advertising and search, as well as targeting ads on social networking websites, you can expect to receive lots of views.

Running PPC advertisements on Taboola is a great method to use your advertising budget, as people pay 53 percent more time to native ads. Many people could benefit from your advertisement through a global network of top publisher outlets.

You already have the experience and knowledge that you need to succeed as a marketing affiliate for dating. Many people still place a high value on relationships and romance, which is why investing in this market is a great way to make money in the short and long term. Because so that the majority of top dating websites invest in their ads, they've already generated a significant amount of traffic, which makes the process of converting customers and collecting fees significantly easier.

Chapter 9: The Stock Market

Stock Market Explained?
The term "stock market" refers to the public markets that are used for buying, issuing and selling shares that are traded on an exchange, or on the counter. Stocks, also referred to as equities, are a fractional ownership of a company and the market for stocks is where investors can purchase and sell their shares of these valuable assets. A functioning stock market is considered essential for economic growth, since it allows businesses to swiftly access capital via the general public.

What Stocks can be traded Exchanges and OTC
The majority of stocks are traded through exchanges like that of New York Stock Exchange (NYSE) or the NASDAQ. Stock exchanges basically serve as a marketplace for the selling and buying of shares among investors. They are regulated by authorities of the government, for instance the Securities and Exchange Commission (SEC) in the United States, that oversee the market to safeguard investors from financial fraud as well as to ensure that the exchange market is running efficiently.

The majority of stock are listed on exchanges stocks are traded on the open market (OTC) in which investors and buyers of stocks usually trade through a dealer also known as a "market maker" who is specifically dealing with the stocks. OTC stocks are those that don't satisfy the minimum price or other requirements to be listed on exchanges. OTC stocks aren't covered by the same regulations for public reporting that exchange-traded stocks are Therefore, it's difficult for investors to find reliable information on the businesses who issue them. The stocks in the OTC market are generally less traded than exchange-traded ones, which means that investors have to have to deal with massive spreads between bid and prices for OTC stocks. OTC stock. However, exchange-traded securities are much more liquid with relatively smaller bid-ask spreads.

Stock Market Players The Stock Market Players Investment Banks, Stockbrokers, and Investors

There are numerous regular participants in the stock market trading. Investment banks manage their initial public offerings (IPO) of shares. This takes place when a company initially decides to go public as a company , by offering shares of its stock.

Here's an illustration to show how an IPO is conducted. A business looking to go public and sell shares to investors approaches an investment bank to serve in the capacity of "underwriter" for the initial stock offer. This investment institution, following a thorough investigation of the value of the company's assets and weighing the percentage of ownership the company would like to surrender through stock certificates will issue the first shares on the market for a cost, and also guarantees the company an agreed-upon minimum cost per shares. Therefore, it is the best interest of an investment institution to ensure that all shares sold are sold at the best price.

Shares sold in IPOs are typically bought by large institutional investors like pension funds or mutual funds.

In the IPO market is referred to as the primary or initial market. After a stock is released in this market in the first place, trade in the stock is carried out through stock exchanges, which is called"the secondary market.. The phrase "secondary market" can be a bit inaccurate, as it is the market in which the vast majority of trading in stocks takes place every day.

Stockbrokers, who might or might not also act in the capacity of financial advisers purchase and sell stock for their clients, who might be individuals or institutional investors. Equity research analysts can be employed by brokerage firms for stock or mutual fund companies. They can also be employed by hedge funds and investment banks. They are people who study publicly traded companies and attempt to predict whether a company's price is likely to increase or fall in value. Portfolio managers, also known as fund managers, such as hedge fund managers as well as mutual fund managers and exchange-traded funds (ETF) managers are significant investors in the stock market because they purchase and sell huge amounts of stock. If a well-known mutual fund chooses to make a large investment in a specific stock, that demand for that stock is usually enough to push prices of the stock up.

Stock Market Indexes

The performance of the stock market is typically monitored and is reflected in the performance of the various indexes for the market. Indexes of stocks are made up of an assortment of stocks that are designed to show the overall performance of stocks. The indexes are traded on the basis of futures and options that are traded on exchanges that are regulated.

Some of the most significant market indexes for stocks include those of the Dow Jones Industrial Average (DJIA) as well as the Standard 500 Index of Standard & Poor's (S&P 500) and the Financial Times Stock Exchange 100 Index (FTSE 100) and the Nikkei 225 Index as well as The NASDAQ Composite Index, and the Hang Seng Index.

Bull and Bear Markets, and Short Selling

Two of the fundamental concepts in stock market trading include "bull" as well as "bear" market. The term"bull market" is applied to an equity market where the value of stocks is generally increasing. This is the kind of market that investors thrive in since the majority of investors are buyers, not short-sellers of stocks. A bear market occurs when the stock market is decreasing in value.

Investors are able to make money even during bear markets with short selling. It is the process of borrowing shares that the buyer does not own from a brokerage company which does hold stocks. The investor sells the shares of stock borrowed on the secondary market and gets the proceeds from the sale of the stock. If the price of the stock falls in the manner that the investor would like and the investor is able to earn a profit by buying the required number of shares to pay back to the broker the amount of shares that they borrowed at an amount that is less than what they would have received from exchanging shares previously at a higher cost.

For instance an investor is convinced that the stock price of the firm "A" will likely drop from its current value of $20 per share the investor can make what is known as a margin fund in order to take out 100 shares from the brokerage. He can then sell those shares at $20 each, at the current rate, which will yield him $2,000. If the price drops to $10 per share, the buyer can purchase 100 shares to give to his broker for just $1,000, and he will earn an income of $1,000.

CHAPTER 10: PRINT-ON-DEMAND

If you're looking to begin an online company but do not have the funds to maintain an inventory of the products, printing-on-demand is a possibility to consider. Print-on-demand's business model is founded on selling the product first, and then producing the final product that can be delivered to the client. There are many ways of printing on demand. There are two primary variants:

1. Utilizing a Print-on Demand Service

These companies typically manage the printing of inventory, printing, and shipping. Print-on-demand services can offer you a variety of printing options. These include various kinds of merchandise like shirts, cups, hoodies, etc. There are many ways to print on the same item.

1. Self-Printing

Another popular option is to buy the equipment for printing yourself, together with the material (paint bags, shirts and so on.) Print when you've made a sale.

Why should you print-on-demand?

There are many benefits to printing on

demand.

Budget The most obvious reason can be that there is no need to need to purchase or produce an item before selling it. You can try out your business plan on a budget that is relatively modest.

Diversification: Another advantage is the ability to print on demand to diversify your sources of income. If you're running a successful company, such as YouTube or a blog, you could create products that are related to your business without the hassle of keeping an inventory.

Speed: Another benefit is the ability to sell your work quickly. For instance, if when a video you've created is popular and you wish to sell a product linked to the video, the print-on demand platform can take orders on the next day when you are able to offer it to your fans. The process could otherwise begin with the purchase of the product before printing and wait for the product to be delivered.

After you have a better understanding of the advantages, let's discuss the disadvantages that this company has to offer.

Quantity: One disadvantage is that your earnings might be lower than when you place an order in bulk quantity. In general, the larger your order, the higher the chance of getting a rare item at the factory.

Naturally, your cost will also be influenced by reviews of the printing service and if you print your own. If you print yourself and you purchase the material in large quantities, you'll be able to cut costs. In the event that you're using an print service and only ordering tiny quantities, your prices might be higher than the self-printer. Another thing to take into consideration is the variance in rates provided by different print-on demand services.

The issue with customizing when using a print-on demand platform is that you'll need to depend on the customization options available. The good news is that a lot of print-on-demand platforms let you upload your artwork.

What is the best way to start?

Let's begin with the scenario that you utilize a print-on demand service to complete the satisfaction of orders.

The first step is conducting some research to identify the right service to meet your needs most. Some of the most popular print-on demand services are Printful, Redbubble, Printify, TeeSpring, and Lulu Xpress. A few of these platforms also marketplaces where you can post every item you sell. Additionally, Etsy gets a special note because, even though it doesn't provide print-on-demand however, it's among the most well-known marketplaces for selling online products particularly vintage items and hand-crafted items. There are many who are able to connect their Etsy store to print-on demand services.

Printful

PRINTFUL has been in existence for quite a while. It allows you to connect your store's online shop to it, which means that it can integrate the products to your store. Orders you place are automatically delivered to Printful and from there they're printed and sent. In addition, for each delivered item, you are provided with a tracking number in the notification.

One of the major advantages Printful can offer is that there aren't any limits. Printful allows you to choose to market a single item or hundreds of items.

If you're trying to market your apparel, Printful is definitely a service you must consider considering due to the choices it offers: you can directly print ink on the fabric, create an all-over print, or even do embroidery.

In terms of charges, Printful doesn't have any charges for sign-ups or monthly charges. The only time you have to pay is when you place an order for the product.

RedBubble

REDBUBBLE is the result of an online retailer as well as an on-demand printing service. Create an online store using the platform to upload your images. You then select the items that you wish to showcase your image and the price you wish to sell each product. Orders are fulfilled by RedBubble via its shipping and printing network.

An online store such as it can help you save costs of the creation of your own store, purchasing a domain hosting, hosting, theme/subscription etc. However, it will mean that you'll not be a part from the platform, which is why it's essential to choose whether you'd prefer to own to run your own shop as well as a service such as RedBubble or even both.

Zazzle

Similar to RedBubble, ZAZZLE is a extremely popular online marketplace that allows users to make a variety of merchandise to offer. Zazzle handles production and shipping, however you can also choose to create these items yourself. Practically speaking you can utilize an online service such as Printful using Zazzle. You can set your own price and you can personalize the items by incorporating your own designs.

Printify

The most notable feature of PRINTIFY is the wide selection of items it prints on. Apart from their free plans, they provide a paid plan with 20% off every item.

Lulu Xpress

If you're an writer, or an author, LuLuXpress could be the best choice. The LuLuXPRESS service is a print-on-demand option for book sellers. The products they the market include Book, Calendar, Comic Book and Magazine. There are many choices of sizes, printing quality and binding.

Selling on an Marketplace (Etsy)

To describe what happens when you sell products on the market and employing a print-on-demand service in order to complete orders, let's take a look at the case of Etsy. Sign-up The first step is the obvious one: register. Visit Etsy.com on your desktop browser (the Etsy app won't work on this site) and then select to select the Sell via Etsy option. The information you have to submit to start an online shop is the shop's name, name, currency the country, the language, and.

Profile to complete the set-up of your store it is necessary to add additional elements, such as the banner and logo of your shop, the about section in which you tell your story, shop policies on returns, payments shipping, etc. Your team members as well as the welcome message to your shop.

Listing Next step listing your items and run your store. The primary goal of listing your items in Etsy is to make them optimized to make them more suitable for Etsy search. The main factors that affect the appearance and placement of items that appear in results of searches, as per Etsy they are:

Relevance of the title and tag The title should be a brief description that you provide for your product, while the tag is the phrase or word which describes the product.

If a search term appears included on both your tag and title of the item, Etsy will consider it as a stronger matching than one which has the search term only in one of the two components. The words that appear at the beginning of the title will be considered more important than words that appear at the end.

Etsy lets you add 13 tags on each listing. Tags that match the exact words that you are searching for in search results in the Etsy searching box will be much better than matching each of the words that make the tag. For instance, for the "pink salt" search "pink salt" Etsy will consider a tag with salt and pink as a more apt match to a tag with only one of these two words. This is a guideline from Etsy on the proper and wrong ways of tag-making.

Relevance of the product's attributes: Etsy wants you to be clear about the items you sell to ensure that its algorithm is able to identify them in the correct way. This includes deciding whether your product should be placed in the vintage, handmade or craft-related categories. In addition to the primary categories it is also important to take a moment to think to which subcategories are most relevant to your list.

Etsy suggests you choose as many precise attributes as feasible. This is essential since it helps your item be seen by a lot of those who shop based on aspects, such as size, event, etc.

The quality of the listing: Etsy offers each

listing an overall score. The score is determined by the possibility of buyers engaging on the page or purchasing. (You can find out more about quality of the listing here.)

The factors that influence the listing's quality the quality of the listing are the thumbnail photo, the clarity of the title of the item, and the attitude of buyers towards the product. The quality score increases when a buyer clicks, saves, or purchases an item upon being shown it in the results of a search. Etsy suggests experimenting with various tags, photos that are updated and advertising on social media.

Market and customer experience in terms of the customers' experience Etsy recommends sellers complete their shipping profiles and provide buyers of the status of their purchases. Etsy also suggests that sellers have an extensive about us page and an area for shop policies that provides useful information about the shop.

The shipping policy you've set will also aid in the optimization for your listings. If you're selling goods within the US You can ask Etsy to prioritize your listings by sending it no cost. Etsy is also a preferred seller for sellers who provide free shipping on purchases of $35 or greater.

Management:

The last step is to control and maintain the shops that you have built.

Seller Protection: The very first important aspect to take into consideration when it comes to managing your shop is the policy for protecting sellers on Etsy. Etsy has specific conditions you must meet in order to be eligible for this protection.

Sellers with protection may be assured that Etsy to assist them with resolving Non-Delivery or not as described cases, and also in looking into charges backs.

Selling Process: A different aspect you'll need to control is the selling process. The details of sales you've made are accessible on your account and in the Etsy application. There are a variety of things to think about. For example, if the amount of the item that you have listed is one item, Etsy will remove that item when it is sold.

Once you have marked an order as delivered, it will be moved into the Completed section. Sellers from Canada, the US, UK, Australia and Canada can purchase and print their shipping labels through Etsy. The shipping options that are available to you will be contingent on the location you are in. The labels offered within the US include USPS, FedEx, and Global Postal Shipping. When the labels are purchased through Etsy the order will be automatically marked as shipped and the shipping date will be emailed to the buyer.

Customer Reviews: A key feature of selling your products on Etsy is the system for reviewing. Buyers are able to review their experience within 100 calendar days following the date of delivery or the estimated date of delivery. (The date of delivery is recorded by the shipping company.) If an order does not have delivery tracking an estimated delivery date can be calculated using the date of purchase along with the shipping days as well as the processing times.

Customers can leave a review of their experience after login to their account. The review may be composed of a 1 to 5-star rating , as well as comments. Your overall score for feedback is the sum of the reviews you've received over the last twelve months. Etsy lets you respond to reviews from customers if you get at least three star ratings from the customer. Etsy lets buyers upload pictures after purchasing. You can choose to conceal photos of buyers.

Processing times and shipping days Processing Time and Shipping Days: The processing time is the amount of time required to deliver an item. If you don't specify an estimated processing period, Etsy automatically sets 5 business days as processing time. The shipping days are the time needed to deliver the order. As the seller, you will have four business days for domestic shipping and 10 business days for international shipments.

Vacation Mode If you're looking to break from selling and promoting your business, you can do this by setting your shop to Vacation Mode. When you're in vacation mode you can set up an automatic email for everyone who calls you. Additionally, you will see an announcement in the middle of the site telling people that you're taking brief break. When you're in vacation mode you are able to edit your listings, modify orders and issue refunds when you need to.

The Etsy App This Sell on Etsy application does everything you need to run your shop. It allows you to make and maintain listings, view your orders and stats and even share your products through social media.

Etsy Print-on Demand with Printful

Integration of your Etsy shop with a print on demand services like Printful is quite simple.
Integration: The initial step to integrate is to sign up for an account on Printful. After you have logged into your account, select the Connect an eCommerce platform option among the options available. When you press connect you'll be directed into Etsy and Printful will ask you to grant access to your store. Once you have granted access and connected your Printful account , you're prepared to print-on-demand.

Etsy Policies: A crucial aspect to be considered here is Etsy's policies on print-on demand products. Etsy requires that you list the service that prints on demand as a producer. According to Printful, you do not have to display them the name of your partner in production in the website of your Etsy shop, and you can conceal this information from your customers.

Drafts: Products you upload into your Etsy store through Printful is saved under drafts. This is advantageous since Etsy charges $0.2 per activated renewal or new listing.

The personalization process: If you get an order that must be personalized, it will appear on Printful with an icon in blue. It is possible to view the request for personalization when you hover over it. To make use of this feature follow the steps provided below.

Shipping Rates: Printful offers four ways to calculate shipping costs. If you're selling only one item, you can view the shipping costs on the product's page. When you're offering greater number or across multiple product categories You can find out more about shipping costs from the following page. If you're planning on ordering several products and would like to calculate the total cost of shipping, Printful recommends that you look through the PRODUCT CATALOG before you buy your products from the catalog.

TIPS FOR PERFORMING Print-on-Demand
Perhaps, by now, you'll have a good idea of the best way to begin using print-on demand. Here are some helpful tips to increase your chances of success.

Customer Selection: An essential, but essential step is to find out the most possible about the clients. The profile of your intended group should include factors such as the personality of the individual, their age, where they live and income, education level job, lifestyle, preferences, ethnicity, etc.

Trends: The latest trends are crucial in the context of print-on-demand. The idea is to search for items that are popular in categories such as home products clothes, accessories and so on.

There are a variety of tools for your research. One of these tools are GOOGLE TRENDS. It will help you determine the amount of interest an item has over time. It is possible to search for it on different timescales, and look up the popularity of social media sites such as YouTube. Of of course, the previously mentioned GOOGLE Keyword Planner tool can help you find trends, too.

Apart from searching your own or using Google's search tools you can also find news publications and print-on demand services that offer valuable details. For instance Gelato's service recommends to be green and stay local by 2021. This is logical given the emphasis placed on protecting the environment and the difficulties of shipping from overseas due to the pandemic.

Customization: A lot of users know where they can get the items they purchase on the internet. These marketplaces are extremely crowded, with many sellers offering similar products. When you design products that are extremely customized will increase the chances of getting buyers.

Think of ways you can tailor products to your customers. For example, if selling products for medical professionals, then you could personalize them making use of the slang every kind of health professional employs as well as using humorous, popular or serious quotes memes, pictures, or other memes.

Communication: Apart from the high-quality of the product the message you communicate in your marketing copy is also important in a significant way. If you're having trouble finding memorable slogans for your product and services, the SLOGAN MAKER free by Shopify includes a set of standard templates that could assist. You can also hire a copywriter freelance from Fiverr, Guru, or any of the other platforms which are discussed in the publication.

Production Time: While establishing the shipping date for your product, be sure that you are considering the time of production. When you select a platform request the production time and alter your shipping time according to your product's page.

Packages: If you see that several stores offer cheaper prices on bulk purchases. Use the same method in your shop too. For example, you could offer discounts to customers who want to purchase 10 items instead of one and clearly state this discount in your price section. This method is particularly effective for products that consumers typically purchase in bulk, like toilet tissue, paper plasticware, batteries pet food, etc.

The importance of samples is even if you're working with a reputable business. Upload your designs and design the exact product you wish to market, and then test the product to determine whether everything is in line with your expectations.

CHAPTER 11: EMAIL MARKETING

Are you aware of the emails getting a lot more and more in your inbox? Yes, there's a person making money from those emails. Marketing is among the few abilities that's going to be around forever. So long as there's something to offer, somebody will pay to be offered for sale. Email marketing is the process of acquiring contact lists and then sending them targeted commercial messages. It can be used to educate, increase sales and create a sense of community for your business. Additionally the use of email marketing is typically an excellent complement to other business methods. But that does not mean that it cannot be used as a stand-alone option. Because of its low initial cost and the possibility of being carried out anywhere, it's an absolute favorite of mine. The potential of email marketing can be observed when you have an item or service you want to market. If you already have one of these, email marketing are a great way to increase sales for new products as well as bring back interest in products that have been in use for a while. For starters, you'll need an email marketing program (EMS) as well as the web page to capture (or the landing page) as well as the email lists. If you don't own an email address, then you can make use of this page as a way to lure clients with an offer that they can exchange for email addresses. It could be a coupon voucher or trial service, an eBook or cheat sheets. Once you've found it to be free and valuable you are able to use it. The choice of the right marketing software you choose is essential for your success and operation. Different programs not only offer diverse features, but also provide different ease-of-use. Review and read feedback from users who have used the program. If the program has an initial trial version, try it for a bit. Freemium EMS such as Mailchimp lets you utilize their services for free with some restrictions. Check out the options and interface to discover what it is that best suits your needs.

Another aspect to think about is the budget. Marketing software for email can be costly depending by the amount of business. If you're an individual, or a small-sized business, it should not cost much. But, the price is dependent on the number people (subscribers) which you've. Numerous factors influence the cost of software, as they typically are available in tiers.

In order to earn a decent amount of revenue from email marketing using your product, you'll have to create automated systems. These can include upsells and cross-sells, abandoned cart reminders as well as promotions. Once they're automated they'll make you lots of cash - money that you'd been missing out on. The best part is that it's an all-in-one setup that requires no supervision. It's so easy to do.

Affiliate marketing means that you sell or promote products or services, and earn commissions. There are many companies out in need of a partner to assist them in selling more products. Look up the most popular databases to discover the products you could sell to your clients. When you're researching ensure that you are aware of all you possibly can regarding the item's intended customers, its viability of the product, and how well-known or sought-after the product is. In the end, you must offer what you would purchase.

It doesn't mean that you sell saddles for horse because you are passionate about horses. It's about selling high-end useful products that you believe that people will appreciate. The most damaging thing you could cause to your income is to muddy it (or to stop it altogether) by selling poor or fraudulent items. Be respectful to your customers and they'll buy anything you offer them. Some affiliate sites to test comprise Clickbank, Amazon Associates, eBay Partners, and ShareASale.

In addition to affiliate marketing, it is possible to advertise and promote other companies through your email. This is usually a once-off payment, and is based on the number of users you've received, you may be able to charge a significant cost.

Depending on your area of expertise depending on your area of expertise, you could also collaborate in a similar way with email marketers from other niches. The way it works is that they be able to share your product with their list , while you promote what they're selling through your list. If you can increase that to a large number, you'll have a lot of people who will click on your affiliate or product link.

The average email marketing professional earns approximately $65k per year. It can differ based on experience and the location, as certain marketers earn up to $100k each year. The amount you earn mainly comes down to the product you offer and how you market it. The majority of people choose high-end items that bring in higher returns per sale. Others marketers choose to sell low-cost products, but earn profit based on demand as well as the volume. It is important to decide what is most suitable for your needs and proceed from there.

When it comes to making profitable income streams that are passive you have many options to consider. In terms of financials, it can be the best choice you make. Making a choice between these income streams will grant you more control and freedom over your daily life than any 9-to-5 ever. All you have to do is to be ready for the investment you make. Although passive income permits you to earn profits without any oversight of your investment, it'll take time and effort as well as cash to begin. The initial costs, if employed properly can make things easier for you in future. This is the thing this article is about, setting up long-term financial equipment that will benefit you and your children to come after you.

Choose a passive income source depending

on your skills goals, as well as your interests. Don't worry if what you select doesn't pay off immediately. Every thing takes time. If you have it set up correctly you'll never need to think about it ever for the rest of your life. Explore your options thoroughly look into the processes and requirements, then get going. Once you're on the right track Find ways to increase the size and maximize your income stream of income. You can even use the earnings in one revenue stream and build another.

CHAPTER 12: Audio Books

"The most ideal time for planting a tree, was twenty years earlier. The next best time to plant trees is right now."The ancient Chinese Proverb

In the previous book, we discussed e-books. They can be a fantastic method to begin an income stream that is passive. Let us look into audiobooks. They've gained a lot of popularity due to our busy life schedules don't allow us to grab an audiobook and listen to.

An audiobook lets users download the book to the smartphone, then put it on headphones and listen to the book while on the go.

However, creating an audiobook is more difficult and more technical than writing an electronic book. If you put your efforts into it, you'll be able to master it with some practice and benefit from the benefits of this lucrative passive income stream.

The good thing is that you don't have to have

all the necessary equipment needed to record an audiobook. It is possible to outsource the task through sites like Guru or Upwork.

In case you're in awe of how to define an audiobook? The basic idea is reading a book read by the author, and having the book read aloud. The author then publishes the book on Audible which is the most well-known platform for audiobooks through Amazon. You might have heard an audiobook. If not, visit the app store of your choice or Google Play and download Audible and try it at no cost. The voice that you listen to reading the text may be the voice of the author, however, it's usually the voice of the narrator who is payed for reading the novel with an engaging tone that reflects the spirit that the text.

How can you become the Audiobook Narrator?

If you're a lover of reading books and believe that you're skilled at narration, then you should start your job as an audiobook narrator now!

It is possible to earn an income that is passive through royalty share or an upfront payment.

The majority of audiobook authors prefer royalty payments due to the fact that they know that if their book becomes the best-selling book and they earn more than one-time payments.

Four Steps to Becoming an Audiobook Narrator

If you've made up your mind, follow the steps below.

* Visit ACX and create an account.
* Choose from a broad selection of audiobooks available to be used for the auditions.

Record your voice while reading the book.

* Submit your recording.

We recommend that you audition for every book you are able to. This will not only assist you in improving your performance, it can also improve the chances of being accepted as a narrator by the author.

The requirements to become an Audiobook Narrator

There is no requirement to have an academic with a Ph.D. to become an audiobook Narrator. All you require is an unmistakable voice and a decent American, British, Canadian and Australian accent. Many authors are looking for narrators of audiobooks with other accents So don't be dissatisfied in the event that you don't have the four accents listed above.

Chapter 13: DEFI (DECENTRALIZED Finance)

Overview

The main benefit of cryptocurrency is its capacity to allow anyone who has access to the internet to transfer money practically anywhere at any time, and without the necessity of a central bank. It's totally trust-free and without limits. Decentralized Finance (DeFi) expands this concept to the next level, allowing any person with an internet connection to access traditional financial products such as savings accounts, insurance , and loans however with much greater flexibility and seamless automation. Now imagine all this and yields that are significantly higher than what banks offers in the present, and you will visualize the amount of money that one could earn.

DeFi, A New World

The cryptocurrency industry is growing at an explosive rate. What began as a revolutionary digital payment method with the introduction of Bitcoin is now turning into an entire industry entirely of its own. The cryptocurrency market exists as a thriving ecosystem, providing cryptocurrency users with various options via the which they earn a substantial cash-flow.

One of the greatest advantages of cryptocurrency, aside from its deflationary characteristics is that it's also untrustworthy and decentralized. The financial crisis caused by the pandemic that is currently in the news proved to be the perfect catalyst to create an economic system.

In its stimulus programs as part of its stimulus plans, government officials from the U.S. government printed trillions of US dollars, making any cash that was in our bank accounts decrease in value. Also, the government lowered interest rates, meaning people who are looking for income aren't able to find a sustainable yield from any of the traditional financial product. This was until they found the high yields of CeFi and DeFi that is the reason for the huge popularity these new products are currently experiencing.

The most well-known and fastest expanding domain in the cryptocurrency market today is DeFi. DeFi stands for Decentralized Finance that is basically a blend of trust-free, programmable financial technology apps and services.

In short, DeFi applications make use of automated contracting, programmable contracts (smart contracts) to create self-executable and open business processes. Also the service- like obtaining an loan is 100 100% programmable, which makes it automated. It means there's no need for a central institution, such as a bank, to divide profits with and also demand things like an excellent credit score.

What exactly is DeFi?

The methods that can be made possible through Smart Contracts are referred to by the name of DeFi protocols. These peer-to-peer lending protocols that are decentralized allow for a wide range of options to earn money from the DeFi market. The most fascinating aspect of this is the fact that this has helped make the borrowing and lending process possible for the millions of people who are not banked across the globe, possibly making them more financially secure.

There are a variety of borrowing procedures, however we won't get into the specifics of how each operate. Be aware that the entire lending and borrowing procedure is similar to the conventional loan structure that is used in the financial industry. In fact, most DeFi platforms have savings accounts. They permit users to put their digital assets like Ethereumin smart contracts to begin earning interest immediately. On the other hand the other hand, those who are borrowers can put digital assets such as Ethereum in an intelligent contract to be used to secure collateral and take out loans at a favorable rate. The money is offered from digital assets such as a cryptocurrency. However, it is able to be converted into any currency one wants, including currency like the US dollar. It's all you need to do is transfer the cash to an exchange like Coinbase.com as well as Binance.us.

In the current time the users have put over $6 billion worth of cryptocurrency into smart contracts. Everyday, people are getting more of possibilities of what types of digital assets they can loan and lend, including cryptocurrency such as Ether or Bitcoin as well as stabilized coins (pegged in relation to US dollar) like USDC Dai and USDC. Dai.

The Top DeFi Platforms

Are you still interested? Let's look at some of the most well-known DeFi platforms out on the market that are making headlines. You'll require an electronic wallet for cryptocurrency that comes with an integrated dapp-based browser. There are numerous different wallets available, but the most secure and reliable option will be with that of the Coinbase Wallet. The Coinbase Wallet is easy to integrate with two Dapps (decentralized applications) which are discussed below.

The most sought-after DeFi applications currently available are currently the MakerDAO platform. Dai is the stablecoin that it uses as its own which makes loans and borrowing processes possible. It is smart contract that permits users to create collateralized debt positions. On this platform, customers can make deposits of

Ether as collateral and receive interest in the form DAI tokens. Due to demand and supply, DAI has allowed impressive rates of 5 to 20% returns for lenders. So, one could earn passive income simply holding and acquiring DAI tokens. Over 400 apps have integrated Dai such as Decentralized wallets DeFi platform games, platforms, and much more. Compound is another thriving digital lending and borrowing app that uses blockchain technology. Like the MakerDAO platform it allows you to lend your crypto to others and earn interest. All you need to do is set up an account with an integrated dapp-based browser, like that of the Coinbase wallet. You can then deposit your cryptocurrency into the Compound smart contract to use it as collateral and then use it to borrow money-- as you would borrow against a home. Many have utilized Compound to get money to purchase the house they want.

Like MakerDAO as well, the Compound contract is able to connect the correct lenders and borrowers and adjusts interest rates in accordance with demand and supply. Then, you're done! The road to earning a huge passive income is just beginning!

How can I buy Cryptocurrency for use to fund DeFi

Before doing anything within the DeFi area you'll require the right cryptocurrency. If you don't own any then you'll have to purchase it through an exchange such as Coinbase and Binance.

CeFi

CeFi provides us with a different option, which combines the best of DeFi and the governance of a central body creating financial products that offer huge returns. Find out more about. We'll also look at the top platforms in this field, Crypto.com, Nexo and BlockFi.

Two branches of Blockchain-based Financial Services

DeFi and CeFi generally comprise two distinct branches of blockchain-based finance. CeFi utilizes DeFi's amazing technology, however instead of being governed exclusively by intelligent contracts CeFi is a centralization.

That's right, DeFi users are entirely dependent on the code that is autonomous. Due to the risk of bugs that could be in that code, it's recommended to stick with trusted, reliable DeFi-related platforms like MakerDao as well as Compound Finance, which are both accessible via your Coinbase wallet. It's also possible to utilize CeFi, which means that investors aren't entirely dependent on code and can count on the assistance of other people. However bad people may be, at the very least they are able to get your money , whereas bad code cannot.

A point to be noted here it is the fact that not

all central exchange (CEX) offers services to CeFi. The top exchanges, such as Coinbase and Binance have embraced the cheap and autonomous characteristics of DeFi platforms. In contrast, CeFi platforms like Crypto.com, Nexo and BlockFi have gained a lot of popularity by offering financing services through which customers can earn interest , or loans for their cryptocurrency. It is possible to even obtain debit and credit cards. Let's review the most well-known platforms.

Crypto, Nexo, Celsius and BlockFi

The way they work is that CeFi systems function like banks, but CeFi is a bank that deals with digital money and does not have an branch. Additionally, the entire business model is built on the blockchain, usually with its own currency that ensures that everything is running. This is what helps make everything more efficient and fluid, with less expenses and higher yields. Additionally, excellent credit scores are not required. The most popular platforms in this field include Crypto.com, Nexo and BlockFi.

According to its site "Crypto.com is the leading cryptocurrency and payment platform." Its platform and exchange you can earn interest on a weekly basis (even 10% annually or more) as well as trade crypto as well as get instant loans as well as swap and farm coins and more. Celsius Network is a similar platform, but the Celsius Network is a similar platform, it has the added benefit the fact that they share their earnings with the owners of its own cryptocurrency.

Nexo BlockFi and Nexo BlockFi are quite similar in that they behave as traditional banking institutions. Both offer savings accounts where stablecoins (cryptocurrency tied to dollar value) US dollar) are able to earn an average of 10% per year (compounded every day)! There is no traditional bank that can provide the same rate at present. You can also get money with competitive rates, and enjoy numerous other benefits.

Starting with the platforms can be as simple as it is. Users must sign up an account with the platform. After completing the necessary steps to prove their identity the user is allowed to transfer fiat currencies (like that of the US dollar) via a bank channel. In other instances the platform will permit the transfer of cryptocurrency into existing wallets prior to moving on. This requires you to purchase cryptocurrency using an exchange.

Liquidity Through Automation

Following the attention the DeFi area has received in the last few months several platforms are coming out with hybrid solutions that combine DeFi and CeFi. The real motivation behind this is the fact that centralized exchanges are currently more user friendly, especially to the technically-challenged. Decentralized exchanges provide more liquidity because of its automation. This is why hybrid platforms bring together the best of two worlds.

Non-Fungible Tokens (NFTs)

There's been some amazing developments created due to the booming popularity in blockchain technology. This includes, of course, the decentralized finance (DeFi) and crypto currencies like bitcoin. But a specific market is expanding by exponential leaps and bounds: non-fungible Tokens (NFT). They represent tokens which are completely unique, and often represent digitally scarce items like artworks and collectibles. Through their presence on blockchain networks, such as those that are propagated through Ethereum, NFTs can be easily identified as exclusive and rare. Furthermore, the owners of NFTs can also help fight copyright infringement. The most well-known use for NFT technology are Cryptokitties in which you can breed and collect virtual kittens. The technology was so popular back in the past that it was close to destroying the Ethereum network. In fact, at one time the most beautiful digital kitten was bought for $170,000! Selling NFTs is the most popular method of earning money, however, read on to discover other options that are possible, such as in the decentralized finance.

Selling NFTs

There are many ways to earn money from selling non-fungible tokens. The most well-known method is to sell them directly to customers. In addition to Cryptokitties and other examples, they also include digital land on Decentraland as well as digital artwork for sale on Nifty Gateway and the rare digital goods that are sold to players by video game developers. In the year 2019 Epic Games, a Epic Games, the publisher of Epic Games made over $4 billion through the sale of a digital product called "skins."

Another method of earning revenues from

selling NFTs is via secondary fees. Video game producers are doing it constantly and fees can be up to 100%. Transaction fees can also be a good way to earn revenue. As the market for this particular niche grows the fees will rise to a higher level.

Create Your Own NFT Artwork using Rarible

NFTs are growing at a rapid rate in the present. Last month, the auction house Christie's auctioned off a digital image of the Bitcoin code "Block 21" for more than $130,000! The artwork is both physical as well as NFT, "Block 21" was designed by Ben Gentilli and is meant to symbolize Satoshi Nakamoto's vision "forged from the exact code that was at the root of everything."

For creating an original NFT masterpiece, make use of this platform rarible.com. Rarible.com is a social network market, marketplace, and an application that lets you create Ethereum-based NFT digital artwork.

You'll need to make your artwork elsewhere, but when you're done, it's simple to upload the artwork (as an JPG or PNG GIF or GIF file) and then click"create" and click on the "create collection" button located on the upper right on the page.

Rarible provides us with two options. Select "single'" if you desire your item to be completely unique and one-of-a unique kind. Select "multiple" If you wish to market more than one piece of this unique collectible. The last step is to select an appropriate subject, an inscription, and the price. It is possible to add royalties to make a earn money if the buyer purchases your artwork again. The royalties of 30% aren't uncommon. Once you have completed this "minting process" has been completed the NFT will be listed through the Rarible marketplace. Other marketplaces for collectibles include Opensea, Knownorigin, Nifty Gateway and Makersplace.

Use Non-Fungible Tokens in DeFi

Debt-free (Decentralized Financial Institutions) has become a hot issue recently, and is gaining a lot of attention within the world of finance. Many experts believe that widespread adoption of DeFi is close to being a reality. Non-Fungible tokens is one sector that is rapidly growing in the DeFi market. Like stablecoins, which are fiat currencies such as dollars, the NFTs are able to be used to represent digital goods, collectibles and even real property. Why not broaden the collateral markets used in DeFi loans to NFTs?

DeFi platforms such as Crypto.com will require collateral prior to the time they will lend you money. The collateral usually takes the form of cryptocurrency such as Ethereum (ETH). Since the introduction of NFTs they can use other kinds of digital asset as collateral. For instance, an art work or real estate property could be tokenized using NFTs and used as collateral for the loan.

Earn Playing Video Games

We've talked about how NFTs are revolutionizing gaming industry online, an industry that generated more than $150 billion of revenue last year , and is growing at an incredible rate. We'll now look into how you can earn money by playing these online video gamesby trading and flipping digital assets that are collected in these games. The majority of the world's players still enjoy traditional video games such as "Call of Duty" or "Civilization" in which the goal is to play-to-win. It's just a matter time until the majority of gamers discover that, on the blockchain, it is possible to play-to-earn.

The Reasons why NFTs Are Valuable in Online Games

There's been lots of discussion about DeFi (decentralized financial institution) in the past year. The current rise in the market for cryptocurrency is due in part to the increasing popularity. However, if the top one blockchain used for online gaming is upgraded to Ethereum 2.0 NFTs, NFTs and the platforms that utilize them are likely to see their value plummet. The market of online gaming and millions of players will be transformed. One reason for this is that gamers can now earn money by winning.

Let's recap. Non-fungible assets symbolize something exclusive that cannot be duplicated, like baseball cards , or other pieces of art. In the digital age they could be tools in games like "Gods Unchained,"" artwork created digitally on Rarible or even land in Decentraland. Digital assets are represented using tokens. By storing these assets as tokens in Ethereum, you ensure that they are protected. Ethereum blockchain you can ensure the security and authenticity of your assets. Thanks to this technology, there's an increase in markets in the gaming world that permit players to sell and trade digital assets, such as rare dragons and swords. Just like on the ground, whether trading comics or stocks there's real money that can be earned.

The primary benefit of blockchain technology and digital contracts in the world of gaming is the way it helps create a stable ecosystem for game developers as well as gamers, in which they can both make money. The advent of blockchain-based games will also provide entirely new revenue models and business streams. Additionally, there will be an economy of the virtual that connects these two, where assets are traded and sold through platforms such as Bakkt.

Earn money playing games that are based on blockchain technology

For decades the video game industry has traditionally been built on a win-win model. The players only played to win while developers earned the majority of the profit. This means that players are able to beat the game numerous times, earn a lot of prizes and other assets during this game but not achieve any real-world worth. But, thanks to game that are based on blockchain, the model of business is now play-to-earn. Today, players can earn real wealth through the money they earn and can collect them in games.

With just tens of thousands of players playing each day, this market has space to expand. But, big names in the industry are beginning to see the potential. For example, Atari is going to create its own NFTs as well as crypto. Ubisoft is investing in research and resources for blockchain-related projects like Sorare. Also, Square Enix is heavily invested in The Sandbox, a virtual real-world arcade.

Top Ten Games: The Top Ten Games

Here's a list of 10 online games that use blockchain technology that you can play now to make money and accumulate important digital assets. Next, in the section below we'll highlight several marketplaces on which you can purchase flip, sell and exchange these digital assets.

1) Cryptokitties. Breed and keep digital cats. "Breed your most sought-after cats to create your perfect furry companion."

2.) World of Ether. Players gather monsters on Ethereum blockchain, and can fight, breed, and then sell for profit.

3) Axie Infinity. It is currently the sole Ethereum-based NFT project with more than 10,000 active monthly users, Axie Infinity lets

users collect the most the most unique fantasy creatures.

4) Chibi Fighters. Combat digital warriors in a virtual battlefield where you can gather and trade weapons as well as other valuable assets.

5) MyCryptoHeroes. Collect, train , and battle historical characters. "Get fantastic extensions and land by collecting or training historic Heroes!"

6) Hyperdragons. Another game that is digitally collectible and built upon the Ethereum blockchain that lets you fight breed, train, and trade your own unique dragons.

7.) Blockchain Cuties. A new game of crypto in which you can play and fight lizards, puppies, bear cubs, and other real and imaginary creatures. Every "cutie" is exclusive and belongs to you.

8.) Gods Unchained. One of the oldest games listed on this list, Gods Unchained is a digital trading card game that grants players the full control over their collections. Also, it offers rewards and tournaments. "The Trading game in which you earns you money to play."

9) Decentraland. It's reminiscent of that of Oasis in the movie/book "Ready Player One." It's possible to live in a digital world that is owned and developed through its user. You can buy plots land and explore the land of others, design and trade valuable assets and many more.

10. CryptoAssault. The game features incredible CGI it is possible to control armies, take over territories, mine resources, and more. Join this massive 3D world filled with hundreds of gamers.

Where can you trade and sell with these NFT tokens?

It is evident above, the most effective way to earn money from these games is to collect digital assets typically as a reward for winning. The same assets are stored in tokens that are traded on Ethereum. Ethereum blockchain. Tokens for the most popular games are traded on decentralized exchanges , such as IDEX, Uniswap, TomoX or on decentralized marketplaces that specialize in NFT tokens like OpenSea as well as Enjin Marketplace.

They allow players to trade/buy/sell any tokens or games items that are collectible. The players can easily make a profit from games, training animals that are tokenized and collecting game-related items and much more and sell them at a lower price using these marketplaces and exchanges. The technology behind blockchain ensures that these transactions are safe and decentralized.

A New Era for Gamers

Since the beginning of humankind we've been enthralled by possessions particularly rare and exclusive items. It could be anything from jewelry made of gold, and baseball playing cards. Today, we live living in a new era that is where the majority of these valuable items are digital and the ownership information can be verified easily using blockchain technology. Gamers can actually have digital possessions, such as puppies and swords. Exchanges can demonstrate the worth of these items.

To acquire these rare, exclusive items, players need to be skilled and innovative. Never before in gaming has there been so much stakes. It's an thrilling time for players.

Yield Farming

As of this writing, the most popular trend in the field of decentralized finance can be described as "yield farming" that is an abbreviation for strategies that involve temporarily putting your cryptocurrency in various DeFi apps that provide huge gains. The majority of these returns don't last however if you manage to have your cryptocurrency in and out of the system in a timely manner and the funds grow, it can work to your advantage. Of course, this kind of investment requires a experienced crypto trader as well as an extensive amount of due diligence.

Chasing Yield

In simple definition, yield farming is a strategy that makes crypto assets be used to earn the highest yields that can be achieved. This can be accomplished via decentralized platforms such as Compound. Every week, the yield farmer could move cryptocurrency around within Compound always chasing which pool has the highest annual return. This may require a move to riskier pools from time-to-time but it is not the main goal when you are looking to make the most of your money.

Yield farmers usually utilize stablecoins such as Dai and the Tether (USDT) and USD Coin (USDC), as they are a convenient way to monitor gains and losses. But, it's also common to generate solid returns with crypto currencies like Bitcoin (BTC), Chainlink (LINK) and Ether (ETH).

CHAPTER 14: CREATE APPS

If you have great ideas that you can transform into mobile applications for users of mobile devices on various platforms like Android and iOS Go ahead and create apps. The growing popularity smartphones has led to the need for mobile-friendly applications. Therefore, you should explore the possibilities in this field and develop an income stream for passive sources.

The fact is that building applications is a coding task and requires you. If you've got the knowledge then go ahead and create high-quality applications that appeal to a broad variety of users. This saves you money as well as other people.

However If you're not a programer, consider outsourcing your programming work to professionals. Focus on creating something unique and how to sell it. Once the pros are finished using the app, you can explore all channels for marketing including YouTube, blog and social channels to Affiliate marketing. It will continue to earn money the duration of time that people make use of the applications.

While outsourcing the coding process can increase the cost of production but you'll make a huge money if your app goes popular. It is important to develop applications that address a need users have come up with solutions for. This will increase your chances of making something useful using the apps.

If you're unsure what to do next Here are some fantastic apps you could consider:

* TRANSLATION Application Many people migrate from one area of the globe to another every year. One of the biggest issues faced by travelers is the language barriers. When they go going on business or holiday, travelers or tourists require an interpreter who can help them understand languages they aren't proficient in.

If you develop an app that can translate to solve this issue, you're well on your way to earning passive income through monetizing your app's popularity via the Google Play Store and elsewhere.

The COOKING App: Many people enjoy trying out new recipes. They want ways to consume healthy and nutritious meals without burning holes in their pockets. Create an app that gives users delicious cooking ideas. Each recipe must have an accompanying recipe guideline for preparation to increase the appeal to users who might be interested.

* FITNESS TRACKER App There is an increase in health consciousness lately. Many people are in a position to remain fit due to the fitness tracker applications that help them to monitor their health. By using the data from the app, they are able to live a healthier lifestyle that improves the health of their bodies and extends their lives.

You can capitalize on this potential by developing a fitness tracker application. It is possible to narrow it to a certain segment of people should you choose. A cross-selling application that is able to meet the requirements and preferences of different customers is an unwise choice either.

* PERSONAL BUDGET App: The growing necessity for wise spending is overlooked by anyone, especially when you consider the economic crisis that is sweeping the globe.

When you create an app for personal budgets that helps people overcome their budget issues. Because this is a widespread issue, regardless of the background, be assured that there is a market for your solution.

* TRAVEL/TOUR GUIDE App The world has been exploding and exploring the world of tourism for a long time. It is a good thing that the trend isn't going to slow down anytime soon. Therefore, you can develop an app to help users get the most out of their travel experiences. Tourists will appreciate this helpful travel tips.

*INTERIOR DESIGN App: This Interior design application will provide users in determining how to improve the appearance and feel of their home. It must be able to give them ideas for design for various house styles and even what you can do with it. The more features you can add to the application will be, the more apprehensible it's going to be.

Based on a Clutch survey Think Mobiles estimates the cost for creating an app to be $171,450. The website states that "a average cost to build an app with the help of experts is

$171,450. The online calculator for app costs suggests the price range as $300,000 and $350,000 for an app that has a multitude of features. Smaller apps that have fewer features may cost from $10,000 to $50,000." So regardless of your budget, it is possible to make an app that promises an income stream. But, what is the best way to make money from your application?

Because of the Internet and the digital marketing you can utilize monetization methods to increase customers to your company and boost your customer base and earnings. A few effective strategies to get back your investment are:

* NATIVE ADVERTISING This is an effective method of marketing. Native ads seamlessly integrate into the application and appear as one of its elements. They are a form of sponsored video or content that is used to advertise a product. Native ads are getting more popular because of the seamless design, which makes app users think it's less annoying.

* BANNERS or DISPLAY ADS Display ads or

banners typically appear in the lower or upper regions on the display. These ads aren't large that they block users' view, rather, they allow users to interact with the app , while also promoting the products or services featured on the advertisements.

* INTERSTITIAL ADS They are pop-ups that are displayed on the screen in particular times. This is an excellent advertising tool for content and messaging apps. It is possible to increase your app's revenues by using this method of marketing.

If you've got an idea or skills, or ability to finance an app that will meet the needs of the demands of users, be assured that you will earn a steady stream of income with the correct monetization strategy.

Remember that in order to create an app for mobile that will be successful it is essential to: Find a specific problem you'd like to resolve using the application.

* Provide the app with distinctive features that can increase its utility.

* Determine your market prior to the time. If you follow this method it increases your

chances to develop a solution-oriented app that will be a hit with your intended people. This is the first step toward earning income through your application.

CHAPTER 15: PASSIVE INSIDE AS using "TIME"

1. Create an eBook and sell it online:
This might sound intimidating at first because it requires you to invest your time in the beginning however, once you have an effective eBook created, you can sell it on the internet. It will generate income streams that are passive for generations. There are a variety of ways to market your ebook, but the most effective and most tested method is to offer it for sale online via an affiliate company such as Amazon or on your own site or blog.
2. Affiliate Marketing:
If you've already got a blog or website already, it's easy to earn an income from affiliate marketing. So long as you've got amazing content and a large audience of visitors to your site, your visitors can earn passive income by purchasing items through your affiliate hyperlinks. The best part is that once you gain a reputation on the internet big corporations will come to for advertising. This

is a great way to generate additional passive income. All you need to accomplish is put in time researching to locate the best product or service you'd like to offer , and then search for affiliate partners within that sector.

3. Content Provider:

You can be an author for websites, blogs or books. Website owners, blog writers and book writers require new and unpublished content they can make use of. You can create an organization to tackle this issue. Create innovative and fresh concepts to ensure that your content is unique, original and has not been published previously. Start promoting your service online and keep an eye out for opportunities to knock on your doorstep. All you have to do is track every requirement, meet it, and then begin checking your account to earn the passive income that you earn from this business concept.

4. Start your own freelancing business If you are planning to establish your own business but aren't certain where to begin you can begin a part-time business as a freelancer in

conjunction with your full-time employee. If you're skilled in web design and development, you can start your web design business off the side. If you're skilled with SEO (Search Engine Optimization (SEO) or social media marketing it is possible to create a social media marketing and marketing company. It can be like climbing a mountain at first however if you are confident in yourselfand commit at least an hour or two each day, you can think of a brilliant concept and begin your own dream company and earn a steady income from a passive source.

You may even decide to quit your job if your passive income is sufficient to provide a decent amount of savings, investments, and to cover your expenses for the month. However, before taking such a radical decision, you must be sure that you're earning steady passive income.

5. Reinvest:

Once you have started to generate several streams of passive earnings, there's no reason to stop keeping your hard-earned cash in savings accounts. Check your investment strategies and objectives regularly. Apart from investing a certain portion on your earnings from passive sources to sustain your business, it is possible to save a portion to fund other investments. I'm highlighting "Reinvestment" as an income stream that is passive as before you use every penny you earn you must be able to plan a long-term strategy that will boost your earnings. You can invest the majority or all of the money you earn in other businesses, real estate or dividend-producing equities, or mutual funds. This can allow you to become a millionaire or billionaire in the future. It's easy to look for investment opportunities that are worth your time in the market, then invest and then earn an additional income from passive sources on a monthly basis.

6. Make an online class:
Do you have a love for some thing or have a technical ability? Would you like to pass on your knowledge to others all over the world,

while also generating a sustainable source of income? Making an online course using UDEMY or any other online education platforms is one of many methods to increase your passive income. However, it requires a considerable quantity of effort and time to create an online class of your own.

There are a variety of topics that could be taught in an online course. I prefer to teach technical skills , such as helping others be successful, selling eBooks Online or learning Affiliate Marketing. You can also choose to teach other areas of expertise like dating sites or public speaking skills. the best way to get ready for an an interview or the language of your choice as a photographer, negotiations and so on.

7.Credit Card Cash Reward Points:

Wouldn't you like in getting money for all the things you're likely to purchase each day? If you're one of people who use their credit card each day at the grocery store, restaurants, retail stores and even coffee shops, you must ensure you have a cash-back credit card that offers better cash rewards for making use of it. I've been able to earn rewards as high as $1000 per year just using these reward programs to meet my everyday purchases.

8. Efficiency Expert

Are you super-efficient? You could leverage your skills to help others' businesses expand. You can approach small-sized business owner and offer to be their sales representative and marketing functions or another part of their business. You could ask the business owner to provide a percentage of the revenue from sales that has increased as a reward for your skills. Once you have started making more money and increasing the sales you need to do is relax and start receiving your earnings. If you start to have regular passive income flowing into your account, you may contact other entrepreneurs and offer assistance to solve their issues and create numerous streams of income by using this technique. It's amazing! Some people who began the service but end up launching their own consulting company and making millions.

9. Run a Class

Visit your community centre, education

department, school or college and ask them to conduct classes on something that you're an expert at. It could be a math instruction, art lesson or yoga class, baking course, or whatever you want to call it. You could even film the class and sell it to thousands of people on the internet. If you're successful in earning passive income through conducting classes, you could start an online blog and sell your items to a larger audience.

10. Sell Your Products or Services

In nearly every aspect of our work all day long, there's numerous ways to generate steady income that is passive. If you're a dietician you could visit patients once or twice every year, but you could create an assessment and diet consultation package that is paid for and delivered monthly or quarterly.

An Yoga instructor's earnings typically be earned by attending classes every day, or for a few weeks or a month, however they could earn a passive income streams by selling products that add value such as herbal supplements which clients purchase each month. You are able to constantly evaluate your particular business, and search for opportunities to tap these opportunities at the right moment to earn a steady stream in passive earnings.

Passive Income Strategies Using "Money" to make an investment 11. The pursuit of passive income through Rental properties: One of the most well-known and tested methods of earning the passive revenue is to invest in an income-generating rental property and then become a landlord. This will require an initial funding and investment (mortgage) and once you have purchased the perfect property, you'll not only earn an income that is regular and steady but you can also earn an enormous profit from capital appreciation as the price of the property goes up. Being a Landlord, have invested in numerous passive income-generating properties, both commercial and residential.

It's amazing to watch the passive income flowing into my account each as well. Every month.

If you do not have enough cashflow transition into corporate life as a full-time employee, or even a business owner Do not be concerned, you can set aside a specific percentage of your monthly earnings as savings for the purchase of an apartment. You can make investments in just one house at a given time and then build your multi-property portfolio over the course of time.

It is crucial to note that if you purchase a property for investment purposes ensure that you purchase it at a time when its price is at a low level or even at a bargain. It is important to be patient and have a long-term view in order to select the best property. In this way, you don't lose money when the market for property crashes and you can have the chance to sell for a higher price during an upswing in property prices.

If your property has a good rental yield each year, it's ideal to keep your investment, and generate rent that is passive.

12. Create an Online Business:

Earning money online requires minimal investment upfront and is able to be completed whenever you'd like. There are many ways to earn money online. Here are some tried and tested methods to make an income that is passive online.

1. Create your own blog

2. Create your own site to sell your products online

3. Online paid surveys

4. Write and publish your books online

5. Sell used items such as clothes, books, CDs and more. on eBay.

6. Create your own YouTube channel on YouTube.

Chapter 16: Waiting for MY SHIP TO COMMENCE

In addition to the possibility of passive income from online social networks, it offers other methods to generate stream of income that is passive. The internet isn't an option as it was ago, and a lot of people who could not prior to now have access the internet. With the advancement of technology and the internet became increasingly accessible, and eventually to the level it is at the present, and is likely to continue to show advancement in the near future. In this section, we'll discuss three other ways to use the internet to generate passive income streams, including dropshipping Amazon FBA, and print-on-demand.

Dropshipping

Dropshipping is the process of purchasing items from a particular source, like an industrial manufacturer or retailer, only to deliver the products direct to customers. It means that you're still purchasing stock but instead of having it delivered to your warehouse, you deliver directly to your client. The process of having real stocks on hand is eliminated completely. There is no need to manage each item that take an enormous amount of effort out of selling. Dropshipping was in existence prior to the advent of the internet. However, today thanks to the internet as an instrument, dropshipping has been easy to do.

Why Should You Consider Dropshipping? Although some effort may be required when using dropshipping, it's not going to be as demanding as operating a physical store which requires the stock prior to selling it. There is no need to verify the inventory, nor will you have to do stock-taking. If a product is defective there is no need to take care of it since it's the responsibility of the seller. Delivery itself is managed by the vendor and is something that you do not have to be concerned about. Dropshipping is , therefore, much safer than running your own shop. It isn't necessary to worry about damage to inventory, losses in stock or even if a delivery vehicle is damaged or malfunctions. It's as simple to find a supplier and then you promote their products.

When a purchase is made then you get the difference between your original cost of the product from the seller and the amount you paid for the item. If you're using dropshipping as a result of running an online store, and don't require purchasing physical inventory prior to making it available for sale, you will not require much capital to begin.

Dropshipping is simply paying for item at the time it was purchased by you. Additionally, because you don't have to keep physical stock You also won't have to maintain or hire the warehouse.

Another advantage of not having to purchase the physical product is the ability to provide your customers a variety of items. If your supplier has an item, you are able to promote the product for your buyers. There is no need to be concerned about shipping, packaging, or tracking the products. New products are introduced to the market frequently. It is possible to use dropshipping as a way to evaluate the efficacy of new products with the least chance that you'll lose money. Since dropshipping companies are typically operated from the comfort of their homes using computers or laptops There won't be a lot of costs, that are typically caused by leasing offices and paying for lots of workers, and having to deal with electric bills in bigger structures.

The most appealing aspect of dropshipping is that you won't be limited to one location. If you're connected to the internet and are able to communicate with your customers and suppliers it is possible to run your business from any location you'd like. You won't even have to drive to and from work. You can work on your own terms making your personal schedule. You'll never be working for anyone other than you, which means there won't be any bosses to nag you. Since your suppliers do the bulk of the work your dropshipping business will be able to grow without needing to do anything yourself.

The Best Way to Set It up

First, you must ensure that you have all the legal documents in order that allows you to sell products. The documents you need include a certificate that shows your company's employee identification number (EIN) that is also known as an Federal tax ID. The potential supplier you are considering will need this as it's an identification of the company. They'll likely require the Resale Certificate. While legal documents aren't demanded by all dropshippers It is highly recommended to dropship legally and in a proper manner.

If you run an online shop You may know the items you want to sell. If not, take your time to consider what products you'd like to offer. Once you've decided on the products you'd like to market it is best to contact directly the manufacturer of these items. Even if a company does not want to use your products, they could suggest a route to help you sell the product. It is also possible to use Shopify to find companies that who you can begin dropshipping with. There's always the option of using Google to find potential dropshipping businesses.

If you're looking for a company that you can do dropshipping with, take your time and don't overdo it. Make sure you do your research thoroughly and select reputable businesses. There are scammers on the market however! If you're cautious and cautious, you can be aware of scams. When searching for a wholesaler or a company you should use modifiers. This means that you must utilize different words in your search engine in order to come up with more results. For instance, instead of just using the term "wholesaler," you can utilize the term "distributor."

It isn't easy to sell a product you've never personally seen. We are fortunate to are able to access the internet! Find out more about the product to find out the specifics of it. You can also read reviews on various sites. This way you will be able to build your knowledge of the product and supply customers with details if they're in need of it. If customers can see that you're experienced in a particular product, they'll be more likely to trust the product enough to purchase it.

The way you market your product is very crucial. Promoting your products in a appropriate manner will ensure that buyers are drawn to it. To make your store more effective, you'll require a well-designed and attractive web site for your shop. The customer experience is of paramount importance. It is imperative to always ensure that the customer feels important and like you're engaged. Always show respect and do not make them feel that they are alone. Be a good example and if you don't show it, it's time to take care! If you care about your clients you will see them take care of you. Keep in mind that dropshipping isn't an opportunity to make money fast. Due to the huge number of dropshippers in existence it is not possible to make a large profit margin. Prices for your items will need to be competitive, in relation to other retailers. Make sure you run your dropshipping business efficiently efficient, efficiently, and with determination and it will be successful in any way you would like it to.

How to improve Dropshipping as a passive income stream

If you'd like your dropshipping venture to be extremely profitable, there are several aspects to take into consideration. It is important to avoid trying to sell inferior products that have an excessive price. Always seek out products of high-quality. Your customers are real people, and they will return the items they purchased when they're not in line with the standards. If items are returned to you to be refunded then you'll lose money. If you don't want your items returned ensure that the quality is in line with the standards. Customers don't want waiting for too long after they've placed an order for a product. Be sure that the shipping service you choose is fast and efficient. Some shipping companies are more expensive however if the service is quicker and more efficient, it's worth the cost.

If your customer purchases an item that will take longer to ship be sure to inform them of it. Don't keep them in the darkness. Be sure to keep them informed on a regular basis assuring them that their item is being delivered. If a customer places an order be sure they are aware of what to be expecting. Inform them of all information regarding the item. Be in constant contact with your clients. If you are deciding on the selling price, be sure to not ignore any hidden fees or costs like charges for credit cards or accounts. Be sure to have everything in mind when you decide about the price you'll sell your products at, especially because you're running an online store.

Be sure to stick to high-quality products you are familiar with. Don't be rushed to sell hundreds of new items that hit the market. Test them a couple at a stretch to determine how the sales are performing. If they are doing well and you're confident you'll be able to believe in the particular product, then continue to sell it. Another method to increase sales is to advertise. Utilize advertising firms to advertise your store and products. Be aware of the items your supplier is low on. Don't advertise on items which are likely to be out of stocks. Promoting a product that's no longer in stock can be extremely damaging to the image of both your business. If you're not sure of what to start to look at, Liz Pekarek (2021) suggests you look into the tote bag, printed t-shirts humorous coffee cups, motivational bookmarks and jewelry which isn't expensive. When you begin the search for items, however you are likely to discover the exact items your shop requires to market. Consider also selling upsells, which are when you offer the customers additional features and upgrades to make a product more appealing. This will not only benefit the client, but also increase your income. It's a win-win! It's time to give dropshipping a shot.

Amazon FBA

Amazon is well known as an, established business that is loved by millions of customers. There are a variety of products available through Amazon. They are often a magnet for people who have business opportunities, and offer opportunities to boost their earnings and assist them in achieving success. In addition, Amazon not only sells tangible products, but also intangible ones. Amazon offers a worldwide service with professionalism and reliable way. It's hard to imagine that Amazon was initially an organization that only sold books, especially when you look at the variety of items they offer in the present.

What are the benefits of Amazon FBA?

With the Amazon brand's reputation and reputation, you don't have to be concerned about their ethical business practices or their relationship with customers or other companies. In the present, Amazon is one of the largest companies within the United States, even compared to Facebook or Microsoft. Its FBA of Amazon FBA can be abbreviated to mean"fulfilled by Amazon. This means that when you ship your item to Amazon it will be advertised and sold by Amazon on their site. They also manage the shipping, as well as any queries from customers following the sale. It is not necessary to be concerned with all of the logistical issues. With all the burden lifted away from you, you are able to concentrate on building a profitable and effective business using this program. Amazon FBA program. Whatever the size and scope of your company is not a factor. If you run a big or small-sized business or even if your product is the product from a hobby that you enjoy You will have the chance to utilize Amazon's powerful structure to boost your fortune. If your earnings are high enough, you may be able to employ staff to take charge of your company. This can give you plenty of time to concentrate on the matters that matter to your most like family, friends and activities that you enjoy.

Additionally, Amazon has truly amazing delivery capabilities. It is safe to say the customers you sell to will get their products faster than if you handled the logistics on your own. Amazon always has a steady flow of customers, so your product will receive sufficient exposure. People shop with their eyes. Visual representations of your product can help significantly in sales.

The number of buyers your product will attract through Amazon surpasses the number of customers you can reach through your online store. As time passes you'll be able to master many of the techniques employed by sellers on the internet. Additionally, Amazon provides resources for the Amazon seller to collaborate with. These include equipment, services and individuals to aid the seller in expanding and grow. Your journey will not stop when you are in a position to sell your items on Amazon. In fact, you'll continue to grow and develop alongside your business. What's not to love about this? But these resources can only benefit the user if they are used. You'll only be doing yourself a favor if you are fully involved and determined to expand your business whatever it may be.

Wouldn't it be wonderful to read the reviews about your product? Positive reviews will only inspire you to improve your product and thus be more successful. The market is constantly in need for top quality products. If you can offer the best quality products that you're confident about, you can be sure that they will be purchased. Amazon FBA will also help increase the credibility of your company by enhancing its reputation. With Amazon managing the logistics as well as customer service it is possible to concentrate on delivering high-quality items that can be a hit and consequently increase sales. Customers love reading reviews of products, as well, and with highly positive feedback of your high-quality products you can be sure that customers will be enticed to purchase the products you're selling.

The Best Way to Set It up

If anyone attempts to convince you that it's too for you to begin Amazon FBA Amazon FBA program, don't take them seriously! It's not yet too late! Amazon is an established corporation however they're expanding and developing each day. You can sell your goods through Amazon and not think that you can't. It's likely to be evident. You'll need an established business in order to sell through Amazon FBA. If you do not already have a business then you'll need to set up a business which you are able to sell in order to obtain all necessary permits, as well as your company's EIN number. Once you've done that it is time to establish a seller central account on Amazon. This is where you'll oversee everything that is associated with your business, like making your product listings and controlling your inventory. If you set up your central seller account you'll be offered two choices for your account: an individual one and an account for professionals. The personal account is intended used for reselling and is only for a short period of time, since it is only permitted to sell up to 40 items.

To sell through using the Amazon FBA program, you have to select an account that is professional. This account allows sellers to offer any amount of products you'd like to sell. You'll have to provide Amazon with the details of your business including bank details as well as credit card information and your government-issued ID tax information, and telephone number.

If you are looking to purchase directly from a seller and sell them on Amazon FBA, you can sign up for an account through an online platform like Alibaba.com. Alibaba allows you to utilize Alibaba to locate suppliers to purchase items to sell through Amazon FBA. There are programs that can be downloaded that can help you find items that have high reviews and are in high demand, leading to significant sales. This software is Helium10. Helium10 includes a variety of tools that will help you locate the right products to market. In the near future, you'll be able to search for items that you can sell. Once you've discovered products that you are looking to sell, visit Alibaba.com and begin contacting suppliers.

If you are dealing with suppliers, ensure that they have trade assurance. That means that if your inventory is lost or damaged, you'll be reimbursed. Prior to purchasing bulk quantities, you should first purchase several samples of the items you intend to offer. By doing this you'll be knowledgeable enough about your product to be able to respond to any questions asked by your customers. Additionally, you'll be aware of what customers can anticipate to receive. Then, you'll be able to determine how you would like your items to be wrapped, making it exclusive to your store. After this then you must get a universal product number (UPC). You will need this code to display your items on Amazon. You can utilize any third-party website, like Barcode Mania or Speedy Barcodes.

Then, you can go back to your central seller Account on Amazon. Select your catalog to add products. The items you add should be ones that aren't available on Amazon. Then, you will select the appropriate category for each item you've added. After you have filled in the information required for each item, you are able to start placing orders with Alibaba. The production process for your items will begin. This could take anywhere between one and four weeks. Following that, set up an order for shipping on your central account for sellers. This can only be done after you've posted the items you'd like to sell.

When you fill out the plan for shipping, you'll be required to input the information for the items you wish to sell, including dimensions as well as the number of boxes. Once you've completed it, you'll receive an address for the warehouse where you have to ship your items to. This address will be passed on to your suppliers so that they can know where to send the items you have ordered. It is now possible to have professional images taken of your items to improve your listing of products. Additionally, you can use time to ensure a pleasing copyright on your listing. Offer your customers details about the product, including why this product is the best choice for them to purchase. You are now set up to be eligible for Amazon FBA (Pak, 2020).

Growing passive income by using Amazon FBA
After you have identified your items and they are ready for sale be aware that buyers prefer to buy items with an outstanding score. They tend to avoid items that don't have any ratings whatsoever. In order to stop this, you can request your relatives and friends to

purchase your items and write a an honest and positive review on Amazon. This can help to start the sales flow. The purchase of sample products for testing on your own could be expensive however, you should make sure that you'll only sell high-quality items. Quality products mean high reviews, which will help you build a image for your company and your brand. The product's testing will help you over time.

You could also think about launching your products using pay-per-click (PPC) advertisements. Amazon offers the choice of brands, products or displays. The main difference between the three options is the place of your product when it's searched on Amazon. To ensure that your product will be found in searches it is necessary to be enrolled in the option of sponsored products. When you use PPC advertisements or sponsor products you'll be able to make an order, and that price will decide where the item will show up when a search is conducted.

To increase your sales, ensure that images used to describe your products are clear attractive, and clean visually. Your description should give the reader the impression that their life will improve when they purchase your product. Therefore, make an effort and you'll get the most amazing outcomes from your hard work!

www.ingramcontent.com/pod-product-compliance
Lightning Source LLC
Chambersburg PA
CBHW071838080526
44589CB00012B/1043